THE PENGUIN CONTEMPORARY AMERICAN
FICTION SERIES

MODERN BAPTISTS

James Wilcox was born in Louisiana and graduated from
Yale University. His stories have appeared in *The New
Yorker* and *Avenue*. *Modern Baptists* is his first novel.

MODERN BAPTISTS

❧❧

James Wilcox

PENGUIN BOOKS

Penguin Books Ltd, Harmondsworth,
Middlesex, England
Penguin Books, 40 West 23rd Street,
New York, New York 10010, U.S.A.
Penguin Books Australia Ltd, Ringwood,
Victoria, Australia
Penguin Books Canada Limited, 2801 John Street,
Markham, Ontario, Canada L3R 1B4
Penguin Books (N.Z.) Ltd, 182–190 Wairau Road,
Auckland 10, New Zealand

First published in the United States of America by
The Dial Press, a division of Doubleday & Company, Inc., 1983
Published in Penguin Books by arrangement with
Doubleday & Company, Inc., 1984

LIBRARY OF CONGRESS CATALOGING IN PUBLICATION DATA
Wilcox, James.
Modern Baptists.
I. Title.
[PS3573.I396M6   1984]   813'.54   83–24994
ISBN 0 14 00.7113 X

Printed in the United States of America by
R. R. Donnelley & Sons Company, Harrisonburg, Virginia
Set in Bodoni Book

To Marie and James H. Wilcox
and
Maud Larson Swift

Modern Baptists

Part

ONE

"Remember how short my time is...."
—Psalm 89:47

One

When F.X. got out of jail, he went to live with his half brother, Mr. Pickens, who lived right next door to Dr. Henry's, the all-night store that sold beer and ice cubes and gas. The reason Mr. Pickens let him live there—it wasn't that big a house, just one bedroom with a den, which was where F.X. slept— was because Mr. Pickens had a mole on his back that looked sort of like a fat New Jersey. At least that's what the doctor said it looked like; he was trying to sound lighthearted so that Mr. Pickens wouldn't feel too bad about the lab report, which said the mole was malignant. When Mr. Pickens heard this, he went numb all over. Forty-one years old and still a bachelor, he had no one to mourn him if he should pass away. So he visited F.X., who was just about to get out of Angola, the Louisiana state penitentiary, and told him he could stay with him at his house in Tula Springs until he got back on his feet again.

Mr. Pickens prepared a big meal to celebrate F.X.'s first night in Tula Springs. It started with a clam dip and Doritos as an appetizer, then went on to mock turtle soup (canned— but Mr. Pickens didn't tell his half brother it was canned, or mock), a tangerine salad with Green Goddess dressing, two huge chuck steaks with candied yams on the side, and finally, a pineapple upside-down cake. F.X. said he was too nervous to eat and only picked at his food. But after dinner he wrapped up some leftovers and took them into the den with him. He said they would come in handy around midnight, which was when he really got hungry.

Out of politeness Mr. Pickens stayed in the den with F.X. for a while and watched TV. It just didn't seem right to leave him alone on his first night out. But it was hard to think of anything to say. He didn't want to embarrass F.X. by bringing up anything that had to do with jail. And he didn't think this was the appropriate time to tell him about the mole on his back—not on a night of celebration. Which was a shame, because Mr. Pickens was about to bust, he needed to tell someone so bad. (*I don't feel anything at all,* he was dying to tell F.X. *I mean, you'd think someone with one foot in the grave would feel a little pain. But it's like I'm all bloated up with Novocain, my hands, my face....*)

"Hey, what's that?" F.X. mumbled, his dark-brown, almost black, eyes fixed on a candy dish atop the TV. Jail didn't seem to have hurt his looks any; he was still as handsome as ever, except for some nose hairs that needed trimming.

"What? That over there?" Mr. Pickens said. "That's some mints."

"I thought I saw a roach. You got roaches, son?"

"No," Mr. Pickens lied. "Care for a mint?"

"Goddamn friggin' roach," F.X. muttered while stretching out a bare foot to turn up the volume on the TV.

F.X. and Mr. Pickens had never been that close, except for a few years when they were children. After Mr. Pickens's father got divorced, he moved away from Tula Springs—where young Mr. Pickens continued to live with his mother—and ran a drive-in theater in Ozone, the parish seat. There Mr. Pickens senior married again, this time an Italian woman who liked saints, which was why F.X. got stuck with a funny name, Francis Xavier. Bobby Pickens was allowed to visit his father on weekends, as long as he promised not to go to the new Mrs. Pickens's Catholic church. F.X., his mother, and Mr. Pickens senior lived right underneath the Ozone Lux's huge screen. Bobby used to think it was the most wonderful place in the world to live because you could stick your head out the living-room window and look up and see movie stars. The ticket booth was connected to the master bedroom, where F.X. and Bobby weren't allowed to play. But they snuck in when their father was away and sold tickets to F.X.'s mother, who pretended to be a gangster. Bobby liked to think F.X. was a pretty good friend when they were young; then in high school F.X. became captain of the Ozone High football team and didn't want to have anything to do with Bobby. Bobby, though treasurer of the Tula Springs High Safety Council and a member of the yearbook staff, had never lettered in a sport.

Halfway through a made-for-TV movie about a widow who learns to care for a broken-legged coyote that maimed her cat, the door chimes rang. "I'll get it," Mr. Pickens said, jumping out of the leatherette easy chair. F.X. gave him a funny look, sideways, so Mr. Pickens tried to act a little more natural as he left the room, shutting the door behind him.

Unable to imagine who would be calling on him at this hour, he was surprised to see when he opened the door that it was the girl who sold novelty items at the Sonny Boy Bargain Store, where he was the assistant manager. She said that she and her girl friend had been driving around, and they wondered if Mr. Pickens would maybe like to go get a Co'-Cola or something.

Normally Mr. Pickens wouldn't have gone out for a drive with her. He suspected that she was more than a little in love with him, and he didn't think it was fair to encourage her. Not that she was all that bad-looking. If she put on a little less eye shadow and stood up straight—and lost about twenty, twenty-five pounds—she'd be all right. No, it wasn't her looks that bothered him. What he found lacking was that certain something that spelled class. He didn't care how much a girl weighed or how many of her teeth needed fixing (that was another thing wrong with her)—if she had class, that was all that mattered.

Although he knew he should stay home with F.X., Mr. Pickens was glad for an excuse to get away from that coyote movie. After telling Burma, the Sonny Boy girl, to wait in the car while he got his coat, he went back into the den and asked F.X. if he minded much if he went out. He said he forgot but he had a date tonight. F.X. said no, he didn't mind at all, and for the first time all evening his face brightened and he almost smiled. Before he left, Mr. Pickens demonstrated how to pull out the sofa bed and explained that the lavender sheets with the tulips on them used to be his mother's, not his. "Yeah, right, got you," F.X. said.

The car, an old Buick with a flame decal on its hood, puffed clouds of vapor from its twin exhausts into the crisp November air. Burma honked when he walked out onto the porch, a four-note honk: "My dog has fleas!" Bundled in his car coat with the imitation fur hood bristling on his head, Mr. Pickens signaled for her to stop flashing her headlights, which might alarm his neighbor, Mrs. Wedge. The four-note honk blared again as he stumbled into a clump of aspidistra in his front yard.

It wasn't until he had opened the passenger door that he saw who Burma's girl friend was: none other than the candy clerk at Sonny Boy, the girl whose watch he had stolen last Friday. Well, he couldn't back out now.

"Scoot over," Burma said to the candy clerk.

The candy clerk, a tall redhead who was something of a snob, said she'd get in the back seat. Burma told her not to be silly; they could all fit in front. Mr. Pickens thought it was a little strange that the two girls were friends, since Burma was thirty-six or thirty-seven—he wasn't sure which—while Toinette, who was new at Sonny Boy, was only eighteen.

Toinette's perfume was strong and made the upside-down cake in Mr. Pickens's stomach start acting up. Burma backed out of the shell driveway in jerks, the noise of the mufflerless engine ricocheting like shotgun blasts off his sturdy cypress house. It wasn't her car, she explained. It was her nephew's. He was being punished for getting his belly button tattooed—not allowed to drive for another month. "I'm still not used to it," she said, slowing down at Dr. Henry's so a car could pull in. "Brakes are funny, you know. And this horn, tacky as sin. I mean my mama nearly died when I picked her up at the beauty college today."

Toinette asked Burma if she hated the new operator at the beauty college, but before Burma could answer, Toinette said she needed some sugarless gum. She had left hers at home.

"Who was that man?" Burma asked, rummaging in her purse at a stoplight. "Mr. Pickens?"

"Oh," he said. He had thought she was talking to the candy clerk. "What man?"

"The man in your house." She handed Toinette a pack of gum. "One stick, now," she admonished her.

"Oh, him," he said. The blinds must have been open; they had seen into the den. Mr. Pickens made a mental note to keep them closed from now on. "Listen, where we going?" he asked, hoping to get her mind off the man. It wouldn't look good if everybody at Sonny Boy found out he was living with an ex-con.

"I don't know," Burma said. "Where do you want to go?"

"I don't know," Toinette said, rearranging her thin, freckled legs on the other side of the transmission hump.

Burma came to a full stop at the railroad tracks that ran parallel to Tula Springs's main thoroughfare. The last time a train had come down these tracks was in 1908, when Tula Springs was an important logging town. But after most of the pine and cypress were chopped down, the lumber company pulled out, and the railroad became nothing but a dividing line between the side of town where Mr. Pickens lived and the side of town where Mrs. Wedge went every Tuesday to pick up her maid.

"Why do you always stop there?" the candy clerk demanded as they crossed the narrow-gauge tracks and turned onto Flat Avenue.

"It's the law."

"Law? Law's for when there's something there to mow you down. Besides, who's going to arrest you, girl?" Toinette was right; Tula Springs didn't even have a police force.

"I still got my conscience," Burma insisted.

When they passed the Sonny Boy Bargain Store, which was dimly lit at night to discourage burglars, Burma honked.

"Don't do that," Toinette complained. "It depresses me."

Next to Sonny Boy was a tin-roofed Laundromat, then three empty buildings, one of which—the old wooden hotel built by the lumber company—had a sign promising that it would soon be the home of Jojo's Health Food Emporium (the sign had been promising that for the past two years). Ajax Feed and Seed, across the alley from the hotel, had all sorts of signs painted right on the cinder blocks in letters that dripped —Purina Chow, Cash & Carry, Mash Spaciel—and if you looked hard, you could see underneath a coat of whitewash, Suck Eggs. After Ajax was a Western Auto and a shoe store that never had the size you wanted. Then came Iota's Poboys, a shack no bigger than a tollbooth on the Lake Pontchartrain Causeway. Finally there was City Hall, the nicest building in

Tula Springs. It dated back to the early nineteenth century, when the Florida Parishes, not part of the Louisiana Purchase, rebelled against Spanish rule. The settlers here, many of them Tories from Virginia and the Carolinas, ate corn, which the French, living just a few miles south, considered pig food. For a short while, in 1810, this strip of land south of Mississippi and north of Lake Pontchartrain pledged allegiance to no one, not to the U.S. or Spain or even England. Mr. Pickens was not very proud of this history—it smacked of Communism. Then, as if Tories and traitors weren't bad enough, around the turn of the century the Illinois Central Railroad began colonizing these parishes with northerners, the shiftless kind that didn't have sense enough to stay where they belonged. It was no wonder that even today there was a certain lack of patriotism in Tula Springs that bothered Mr. Pickens. The state had condemned City Hall, and for good reason: Although it was admittedly a handsome old building (after several fires it ended up being Greek Revival with twelve stately columns), it was downright dangerous. The Commissioner of Parks and Sewers' high heel had poked right through a rotten step on the winding staircase, causing a nasty fall that made her forget who she was for a week. But the mayor, whose grandfather was born in Iowa, refused to budge from the condemned building, which made the whole town seem slightly illegal to Mr. Pickens.

"Let's go to Junior's," Toinette said after they had driven a few minutes and were passing the Tula Springs Hatcheries just outside the city limits.

"Maybe I should be getting back home," Mr. Pickens said after gazing absently at the long row of automated coops. At the edge of a pasture a scrawny, twisted tree leaned into the starless sky, which seemed dense enough to support it.

"Party pooper," Toinette said.

"Don't call Mr. Pickens a party pooper," Burma said. "I know he really wants to have a Co'-Cola with us. Don't you, Mr. Pickens?"

Mr. Pickens didn't. "Well, just one," he said.

CHAPTER

Two

Junior's was off the highway at the end of an unpaved road that cut around a dried-up pond where they used to farm catfish. There was no sign on the plain, sagging building, no windows either, which was a shame, because the view would have been nice. Tula Creek broadened here, leaving behind the eroding banks of vine-tangled river birch to ripple past a beach of white sand and gravel.

After parking the car Burma took off her platform shoes and told the candy clerk she'd better do the same if she didn't want her ankle twisted. But without waiting for Burma, Toinette marched right ahead, the sand crunching under her high heels like snow.

"She won't listen," Burma said, holding the screen door to the bar for Mr. Pickens while he knocked the sand out of his loafers.

At first they couldn't see anything inside, even though there were colored lights dancing and twirling over the bar. But when their eyes adjusted to the dark, they spotted the candy clerk sitting in a booth by herself. She was already ordering a drink from the waitress.

Mr. Pickens sat on one side of the booth, while Burma slid in next to Toinette. Toinette told Burma she had a smudge under her eye, and Mr. Pickens began listening in on the conversation in the booth behind him. A woman was saying something about a metal guard she had ordered for Bertha, to keep her from pecking the pullets. It fastened right on her beak. The man with her said it wasn't Bertha's fault; Bertha probably wasn't getting enough protein. "Feathers are all protein," he said. The woman said something back, but Mr. Pickens didn't catch it because the jukebox went on.

"Isn't it?" Burma asked, laying a rough palm on his forearm.

"Isn't what?" he asked, gently removing his arm.

"Isn't it Mississippi on the other side of the river?"

The waitress arrived with three drinks and set them down. Mr. Pickens told her he hadn't ordered anything yet, but Toinette told him to relax. She had ordered to save time.

"What is it?" he asked, testing the drink with a tiny sip.

"Tab cola," Toinette replied.

"It doesn't taste like Tab."

"They might have put a little bourbon in it."

"That's Toinette's drink," Burma explained to Mr. Pickens. "Toinette won't drink nothing but bourbon and Tab cola, will you, Toinette?"

Toinette nodded as she sipped the drink through a dainty straw. Her nostrils flared.

Burma asked again if it was Mississippi on the other side of the river, and Mr. Pickens said no, the state line was about a mile upstream.

"That will be one dollar, miss," Toinette said, holding out her hand to Burma. "I told you it wasn't."

Now that he found out Toinette was winning a bet, Mr. Pickens wished he hadn't told the truth about Mississippi.

He'd much rather have seen Burma win. The way Toinette always looked at him, like she was the queen of England, made him wonder if she realized that at any moment, just like that (he mentally snapped his fingers), he could have her fired. It would be easy as pie.

"What time is it?" Toinette asked.

"What do you have to know the time for?" Burma asked. "We just got here."

Toinette looked down at her bony wrist, where her watch used to be. Mr. Pickens's round, boyish face turned red, but with all the colored lights flashing he just ended up looking a little more purple.

"I always like to know what time it is," Toinette said.

Mr. Pickens took a few gulps from his drink. He really wished he hadn't stolen Toinette's watch last Friday. It had started out as a practical joke—an icebreaker, really. He had been thinking of ways to get to know the candy clerk better, and then on Friday he noticed that for some reason she had left her watch next to the pecan Turtles. It was the perfect opportunity. While she had her back turned, weighing out some Candy Corn, he nonchalantly walked by and palmed the watch. The point was to get her nervous and excited, then produce it suddenly and make her laugh at herself for getting upset over nothing. The technique had worked once before for Mr. Pickens, not at Sonny Boy but over at the mall in Mississippi when he was working as a shoe clerk. The shoe clerk he had stolen a bracelet from hit him with her fist when he gave her back the "stolen" jewelry. Of course it didn't hurt, and she decided he was more interesting than he looked and let him take her to the movies. Mr. Pickens had no intention of ever dating Toinette (she was both too young and too tall), but he did want her to know that he wasn't a stuffed shirt like some people thought. Unfortunately the scheme failed.

When the candy clerk saw her watch was gone, she tore like fire to the back of the store, where the manager and Mr. Pickens shared an office. Mr. Pickens tried to catch up with her, but by the time he got to the office, she had already told Mr. Randy, the manager, who then called in the security guard. Mr. Pickens couldn't explain now. He could only wait for a chance to sneak the watch into Toinette's purse, and hope she would think she had put it in there by mistake.

"Look, Mr. Pickens finished off his Tab," Burma said. She waved at the waitress, then made a circular motion with her hand over the table.

"I don't care for another," Mr. Pickens said.

"See, I told you he was a party pooper," Toinette said. Then she told Burma to move so she could go freshen up.

Burma and Mr. Pickens were left alone for a few minutes while Toinette went over to the bar and started talking to Junior. Mr. Pickens kept on glancing over his shoulder at her. If a person said she was going to freshen up, then she ought to go freshen up, not stand around talking forever. Junior, a fat old man who claimed he never ate anything in his entire life but hamburgers, even when he was a baby, caught Mr. Pickens's eye. Mr. Pickens looked back at Burma.

"Don't be mad at Toinette," Burma said, snapping the rubber band on her wrist.

"I'm not mad at her."

"You look mad. And why don't you take off that thing? Here." She leaned over the table and began to unzip his car coat. He removed her hand and began unzipping himself.

"Oh, let me see," she said.

"What?"

She reached for his left hand and examined the amethyst in his class ring. "Bless your heart, St. Jude. I didn't know you went there," she said, releasing the hand. An hour from

Tula Springs, St. Jude State College's small, idyllic campus looked right out on Lake Pontchartrain. Everyone from Tula Springs High went there, except for a few brains who went to L.S.U. "When did you graduate?" she asked.

"I was in the class of 1963," he said, avoiding a lie. He did not feel like telling her he hadn't graduated but had dropped out in his junior year because he hated living in a dorm. Everyone was always snapping rattails at you in the shower.

"Then you must have been there when I was there. I'm '66, that's when I graduated, 1966."

"Really," he said, trying to mask his surprise.

"Got a B.A. in sociology. My teacher wanted me to go on and get my master's. I said fine, I will, but I'm not going to do any paper longer than five pages. I just hate papers; they make me want to quit living. So my teacher says to me, 'No, ma'am, you got to do long papers just like everyone else,' and I say, 'Suit yourself, been nice knowing you.' What did you major in, Mr. Pickens?"

"Agricultural sciences."

"You mean, you wanted to be a farmer?"

Mr. Pickens had never wanted to be a farmer. He had enrolled in the Department of Agriculture, though, because at the time he was mad at his father. His father thought that becoming a farmer was about the worst thing that could happen to someone. Growing up, Mr. Pickens was always being told to stop talking like a farmer, stop dragging his feet like a farmer, stop thinking like a farmer. So when Mr. Pickens went off to school, he got his revenge. The only problem was that being an aggie major was harder than he expected, and he wished he could be something easy, like an English major.

"I was more into the technical side of agribusiness," Mr. Pickens said in reply to Burma's question.

Burma sat there a moment, a blank look on her face. While

Mr. Pickens tried to think of something else to say, Toinette returned to the table and, after groaning loudly, said she wished she didn't have to go to work tomorrow. Her feet were killing her. "They ought to make it where you can sit while you work," she went on. "I don't see any reason why we got to stand all the time."

"That's what I like about Mr. Pickens," Burma said. "He never reports me when I sit down."

"Well, he better not report me," Toinette said, looking right at him, " 'cause I plan to do some sitting tomorrow."

"Now, listen, girls," Mr. Pickens said as a long strand of blond hair drooped down his nose; he shoved it back up on his balding pate. "I got to treat y'all like everyone else at work and . . ."

They lost interest in what he was saying, though, and began talking about Mr. Randy's lime-green pants, how much they hated them. Toinette's flat, almost Oriental face was wrinkled in disgust. It was strange, he thought, how she could look beautiful one minute, ugly the next, depending on the angle.

"Who was that man at your house?" Toinette asked after the waitress brought them the check. Even though Mr. Pickens insisted on paying, Burma made him put his VISA card away. She said she and Toinette were treating. And besides, they didn't take VISA at Junior's, only cash.

"Who was that man?" Toinette persisted when they had finished figuring the tip.

"You already asked him that," Burma snapped. "And I done asked him once myself." She dabbed at her lips with a tube of white lipstick. "He would've told us if it was any of our business."

"So what's the big secret?" Toinette asked, patting a failed frizzy redhead version of the elaborate Farrah Fawcett hairdo.

"I don't like that chocolate-colored shirt Mr. Randy wears,"

Mr. Pickens said, trying to veer the conversation back onto a safer topic.

"Is he a friend?"

"We don't really socialize much, Mr. Randy and me."

"No—the man in your house."

Mr. Pickens had to say something; they were getting too suspicious. "He's my uncle. Just visiting."

"Uncle? He's mighty cute for an uncle."

"Toinette, quit bothering Mr. Pickens."

"I'm not bothering him. I just think it's strange that an uncle looks younger than his nephew."

Mr. Pickens didn't realize she had got such a good look at F.X. She must have eyes like a hawk. "Well," he offered lamely, "there's been a lot of divorce and all in my family."

" 'And all' is right," Toinette said.

"Okay, girl, you asked for it." Burma slipped the rubber band off her wrist and shot it toward the bar. "Toinette spied on you, Mr. Pickens. When you went back inside the house for your coat, she—"

"Hush," Toinette said.

"She ran up to the bushes under your window and peeped in. I told her it was wrong, but she— Ouch!" Burma slapped Toinette, who had pinched her on the arm.

"Oh," Mr. Pickens said. He really didn't care that much anymore. So let them find out he was living with an ex-con. Did it really matter? After all, he was going into the hospital next week, and there was a good chance he might not come out alive. How could he have been dumb enough to forget this? Yet he had—for a while, at least, sitting there listening to them talk about lime-green pants and aching feet.

"Why didn't you tell your uncle to come?" Toinette said as they all stood up to leave. "We could've been four, then. Burma, don't wave at Junior. You know he likes you."

"He does not," Burma said, waving.

"Junior's got a crush on Burma," Toinette whispered to Mr. Pickens as they stepped outside. The fresh air, laden with the rich smell of soil from the river, made him feel less woozy.

"What did she say?" Burma asked Mr. Pickens.

"I told him the *truth*," Toinette said and then dodged as Burma's handbag grazed her shoulder. Laughing, Burma took aim at her girl friend again and hit Mr. Pickens on the mouth with the bag's metal clasp. It stung, but it wasn't worth mentioning.

"Tell her to stop hitting me," Toinette said, holding on to Mr. Pickens's arm and using him as a shield.

"Now, girls," he cautioned.

The moon, rising over the river birch, seemed to tug at Mr. Pickens's heart. He was a shield for a little while longer, then herded the girls into the car. It was time to go home.

CHAPTER

Three

Mr. Pickens knocked softly on the door to the den before poking his head inside. "Can I come in?" he asked, then winced as Burma's four-note honk blared from the driveway; the girls were driving away. F.X. was propped up on the pull-out sofa, gnawing on a steak bone while the TV played. It was a deluxe model with a carved blond cabinet, and F.X. had moved it from its accustomed place next to the radiator so that it would be closer to the bed. Mr. Pickens noticed a big dent in the shag rug where the TV was supposed to be.

"Everything okay?" Mr. Pickens asked.

"I can't get the remote control to work," he said, holding up the brown box. F.X. had a very distinctive way of talking. Instead of his lips, which barely seemed to move, it was his eyebrows that did most of the work, raising or lowering, separately or together. It was a little disconcerting.

"Remote doesn't work with cable."

"So Tula Springs has got cable." F.X. wrapped the bone in tinfoil and set it aside. In his white boxer shorts he looked like he had just got back from a week at Biloxi. But it was his olive skin, not the sun, that made him look so tan. And he was fit too, astonishingly fit. As Mr. Pickens went to the window and pulled down the venetian blinds, he tried to suck in his paunch.

"We just got it," he said, wrapping the cord around a window crank. "We get Baton Rouge, New Orleans, Houston, Atlanta, Alexandria." The shadow of his round head rose up on the dark knotty-pine wall; he switched off the Danish modern lamp, and the shadow vanished.

"I saw myself," F.X. said. In the flickering light of the TV he seemed to hover over the lavender sheets, barely touching them. "Remember that commercial I did in Baton Rouge a few years ago? You know, the car wax thing where I'm kissing the hood? Yeah, well, it was on tonight."

F.X. used to get some television work, as well as a few assignments modeling clothes for Maison Blanche catalogs. But his real aim in life was to be a celebrity—preferably a film star. For the past twenty years he had been drifting back and forth between New York and Los Angeles, returning to Louisiana whenever he was hard up for cash. The last job he had, before being sent off to prison, was in a revival of *Come Blow Your Horn* at a dinner theater near Ozone. Although he had a starring role, they made him sing a song in between the acts pushing the house drink, Cajun Catnip. It was a choice between singing the song, which he hated, and waiting on tables—so he sang. All this had come out at the trial two years ago, which was how Mr. Pickens knew about it. Generally F.X. was vague about his career.

"No residuals," F.X. said after his brother asked him whether he shouldn't get paid for the car wax rerun. "I got a flat fee, a hundred bucks."

"You never did have a good head for business," Mr. Pickens commented, and instantly regretted it. He was afraid F.X. might take this as an allusion to his arrest: F.X. had been caught selling cocaine at the dinner theater to the special guest star from London. "I mean I've always thought of you as the artistic type."

An eyebrow was raised.

Mr. Pickens coughed, then picked out a mint from the candy dish.

"Say, Bobby, you ever hear from that fuck?"

"Who?"

"The old goat."

"Oh." Considering a moment, he said, "Dad's fine." Of course their father was not fine. Shortly after F.X.'s trial Mr. Pickens senior had declared he couldn't stand one more minute of Louisiana. So he sold the drive-in, and in lieu of going to the moon—which was the only place he could think of that wouldn't have any trees or grass or swamps or anything else that reminded him of his native state—he and his wife resettled in Tucson. There his wife, F.X.'s mother, was accidentally run over in a Burger King parking lot. Mr. Pickens junior wanted to go out for the funeral—after all, F.X.'s mother had always been kind to him; and also he would have liked to see what the West looked like in real life—but his father forbade him to come. He said he never wanted to set eyes on Bobby again until he got married.

"Just fine," Mr. Pickens repeated.

"You know what that bastard did? Waited till a week after the funeral. Then he tells me about her. I get a postcard at Angola, he sends me a fucking postcard."

"F.X., he's old. You can't . . ."

" 'Your mother's dead,' he says. 'Hope you're satisfied.' That's how I find out about it. 'Hope you're satisfied.' I like that."

"He's old."

"He's old, he's old," F.X. said wearily. "I'm old, you're old, we're all old. That doesn't give anyone the right to say things like that."

"No, but . . ."

"Cool it, son. I don't want to talk about it."

Sliced by the half-closed venetian blinds, a car light rippled over the foot of the bed as someone pulled into Dr. Henry's next door. Mr. Pickens went to the window and closed the blinds tight. A car door slammed; voices. It sounded as if they were standing right under the window. "He's weird, man," one teenager kept repeating while another talked non-stop. "And then, oh, yeah, right, then he says to me, I ain't doing none of your fucking homework for you, and I say, wow, you got to be kidding, I never said . . ."

"Yeah, we're all old," F.X. said over the voices. He sounded calmer now. "You realize, son, that in ten months and twenty-four days I'll be forty?"

Mr. Pickens sat tentatively on the window seat.

"Scares the living shit out of me," F.X. went on while staring at the TV, which was still on, the volume low. "I sometimes wake up in a cold sweat thinking about it. Forty and a nobody. Hell, I'd rather be dead."

"Well, now, listen, it's not really so—"

"At Angola I once woke up screaming, thinking it had already happened. Buster, my cell mate, he had to splash cold water on my face. Yes, sir, I'd rather be dead, dead as a doornail. 'Cause there's no way I'm going to be a nothing, not a forty-year-old nothing."

"Don't you think you're . . ."

His eyes still fixed on the set, he said softly, as if to himself, "Been counting the days, boy. Ten months, twenty-four days . . ."

"Twenty-three," Mr. Pickens corrected. It was five minutes after midnight.

"What?" F.X. said, looking annoyed. He punched his pillow and got under the blanket.

"You know, F.X., I think about things too. Serious things, I mean."

F.X. reached out a smooth bare arm and switched off the set. He yawned loudly.

"People don't really like to talk about serious things," Mr. Pickens said, leaning back in the window seat. "Like no one ever asks me about my mother anymore." Mr. Pickens's mother was in a nursing home, over in the next parish. F.X. knew this but never once asked after her health. The bedsprings creaked as F.X. changed positions.

"Things like death and all," Mr. Pickens said to the darkened room. He wanted to yell out the window to shut those damn kids up; it was hard to think with all that yakking going on. But kids nowadays had a real mean streak in them. There was no telling what they might do if you stirred them up. "People get antsy if you start talking about it. It's a shame, because I think about it a lot. I'm always wondering what it's going to be like afterwards." He scratched a rash on his arm; the doctor thought it was an allergy to something, but he wasn't sure what. "It's funny, but the whole idea of heaven scares me just as much as hell. I guess the thought of living forever, me up there forever—even if it doesn't hurt, even if it feels good and I'm happy all the time—still, it's just too much. Then I think, okay, so maybe when you're dead, you're dead, and there's no more you. I try that one out, and Lord, F.X., that one scares me just as much. I mean, what if it's true what some people say, that there's not going to be any Last Judgment? Doesn't that seem just about as awful as if there *was* going to be one? Think of people like Hitler and Nero and Castro, all of them getting off scot-free."

Mr. Pickens paused. The Last Judgment: he would have to get that watch back before he died.

"F.X., you ever wonder if you want to be you forever? F.X.?"

Mr. Pickens felt his way quietly to the other end of the room, nearer the bed. "F.X., you awake?" He squinted down and saw that his brother's eyes were shut.

In his bedroom at the rear of the house Mr. Pickens paused before the mirror on his chest of drawers. His brown tie was crooked; the brown jacket hung wrong on his shoulders. He tried standing more erect, making the shoulders less rounded, but still the jacket looked cockeyed. He got undressed, leaving his double-knit pants in a heap on the floor. After placing his contact lenses in a solution in the bathroom sink, he turned and looked at the scar on his back where the mole used to be.

Lying in bed with the electric blanket turned up to eight, he heard Johnny Carson's voice coming from the den, loud and unashamed.

CHAPTER

Four

When Mr. Pickens got home from Sonny Boy the next day, F.X. was on the hooked rug in the living room doing push-ups.

"Sixty-one—hi—sixty-two," F.X. gasped; he slapped his chest hard on each upstroke.

"Hi," his brother replied, unclipping his tie and tossing it onto the love seat. He went into the kitchen and made himself a screwdriver. Usually he drank two or three of these before he felt relaxed enough to eat. This evening he poured an extra dose of vodka into the drink. The nurse at the doctor's office had called him today at work and told him that there had been a little mix-up. The spot he had on his back, the one that looked like New Jersey, well, it wasn't malignant at all. The lab in Ozone had bollixed things up. They were having trouble with their computer, and so his specimen got the wrong identification number on it. The nurse said she was real mad at the lab, but there was nothing she could do about it. She said the doctor was mad too. Then she told Mr. Pickens he ought to be real happy. Nothing was wrong with him.

Mr. Pickens finished the first screwdriver quickly and fixed himself another. He couldn't figure out why he didn't feel happy. Here he was, knowing that he wasn't going to die after all, and he felt pretty much the same.

"Like a drink?" he asked, standing in the archway that led into the kitchen. Above him dangled macrame tassels, the handiwork of a former girl friend who had ended up marrying the new civics teacher at Tula Springs High.

F.X. was on his back now, doing leg lifts. "Come here, son. Do a few with me. It'll tighten up your gut." He yanked up his Alligator shirt and slapped his stomach. It was impressive, all right—a classic washboard stomach.

"Maybe later."

"Listen, Bobby, that plastic on the love seat, it's got to go." The legs scissored wide and knocked against the carved lion's paw on the love seat's armrest.

"I already tried," Mr. Pickens said. The clear vinyl on the love seat had been his mother's idea of a birthday present. She was still living with him then, back before her wallpapered bedroom had been converted into the wood-paneled den. As a surprise for his thirtieth birthday she had some men from Ozone come in and vinylize the love seat and davenport, the overstuffed wing chair, and the embroidered armchair while he was out working at the mall. He lived with it for a year. But as soon as she was admitted to the nursing home, he very methodically devinylized the living room, all except for the love seat, where the vinyl had actually melted into the material and could not be removed.

F.X. came into the kitchen as Mr. Pickens was finishing his third screwdriver. Mr. Pickens said he had bought some TV dinners for tonight; that's what he usually ate when he was alone. F.X. was in the mood for something more exciting, so he looked through the cupboards to see what his brother had in store. There were instant mashed potatoes and two cans of sardines.

"I'll run over to Dr. Henry's," F.X. said.

A few minutes later he returned with some frozen veal patties. "Frying pan?" he said, tossing the patties onto the counter. Mr. Pickens said he'd cook, but F.X. reminded him that he had cooked the night before.

"I saw the old homestead today." F.X. cut a stick of margarine in half and put a piece in the skillet. "The drive-in is still standing there, but all the speakers are ripped out. There's just the big screen staring out at the lake. It's sort of neat."

"You mean you went to Ozone?" Mr. Pickens said. He was getting used to F.X.'s way of talking, just barely moving his lips.

"I forgot to tell you this morning. I took a meeting with Mike today, my parole officer. He's in the courthouse there." An eyebrow dipped. "Mike wanted to know all about you, Bobby, so I told him how respectable you were and how you weren't going to let me get away with anything. 'Does he have a record?' Mike asks me, and I say, 'You kidding? He has plenty of records, all bad. Like there's Mantovani, The Four Seasons . . .' "

"F.X., maybe you shouldn't joke like that."

"To Mike? He's regular, son." He picked up the box of instant potatoes and studied it a moment. "Saucepan. You got a saucepan? No, sit. I'll get it. Just tell me where."

"Bottom cabinet, the other, next to the stove."

Going to the refrigerator for more orange juice, Mr. Pickens collided with his brother and spilled part of his drink on the flowered linoleum. F.X. tossed a dishcloth onto the puddle and swished the cloth around with his foot.

"Don't worry about that," Mr. Pickens said, pouring vodka into his glass. "By the way, how did you get to Ozone? Is there a bus or something?"

F.X. was working his jaws like he had gum inside—only he didn't. "Drove. Figured you wouldn't mind."

"Drove what?" Mr. Pickens went back to the dinette table and sat down again.

"The car."

"What car? You mean my car? I took my car to work today."

"No problem. I just trucked on down to Sonny Boy and got it. I mean, I looked around for you—must've gone up and down those aisles about fifty times. Then this chick stops me and says you've gone out to lunch. So what am I supposed to do? I *had* to get to Ozone or my ass was busted."

"No, you need a match to light the stove. In the drawer to your right." Mr. Pickens sipped his drink. "F.X., I had the keys."

"You have an extra set, remember?" He got the matches and lit a burner. "I found them on your chest of drawers."

Mr. Pickens thought he should establish a house rule right here and now concerning snooping. "So you saw the old drive-in," he said instead. "Ozone Lux."

"You know, son, you wouldn't make a very good detective."

"What?"

"Your car. When I brought it back, I couldn't park it in front of Iota's, where you had it. I ended up a block away, and you didn't even notice." He tapped a spoon rapidly on the edge of the saucepan, waiting for the milk and water in it to boil.

"Remember that time we climbed up on the screen?" F.X. said as margarine spattered out of the frying pan. "Dad wanted us to scrub that black mark off, and I was holding the ladder for you. Next thing I know, I got this blood blister where the ladder squeezed my thumb." He tossed a frozen patty into the skillet; at the table Mr. Pickens was stung by hot grease. He told his brother to put a lid on the pan.

"Then remember the time Dad wouldn't let us see that film

with Mamie Van Doren in it?" F.X. said after finding a lid. "We're lying there in bed, and you say maybe if we unscrew the light bulb, we can see through the ceiling. We knew she was up there, this fifty-foot Mamie Van Doren, and we knew she was doing stuff we weren't supposed to see. I did an improv on that once."

The milk suddenly boiled over onto the burner, making the flame hiss yellow. "Turn it down," Mr. Pickens advised.

F.X. picked up the box and looked at the directions again. "Pepper," he said, moving the pan to another burner. "So anyway, this improv I did for an acting coach I had in New York, Mr. Schlemiel or something. He'd make us dredge up all this shit from our childhood, said we could never be actors till we remembered everything. I tried real hard to remember something good, but it wasn't easy, man. Then all of a sudden it comes to me, this night with Mamie Van Doren up there, so I get up and start acting it out in front of the videotape machine. It was weird, really weird, 'cause halfway through my spiel I start becoming you instead of me. I mean, it was sort of boring till I started getting in your shoes. Then it got heavy, real heavy, and I began spouting all this stuff about how everyone in high school hated me and how I—"

"Everyone didn't hate me."

"Well, Bobby, you did hang out with losers, you got to admit. Anyway, then I go on about how my brother was this big football star, really good-looking and all, and I start saying how much I wished I could be him because—"

"I never wished I could be you."

"—because he got all the girls, and how one day this Mamie Van Doren would come down off the screen and electrocute him and everyone else who—"

"Electrocute?"

"It's free association—you're supposed to say whatever comes into your head. Hey, listen, man. Don't look at me like that. My acting coach thought it was fucking good. He said it was deep."

"It's deep, all right."

"I suppose you could do better."

Mr. Pickens gazed absently out the sink window. The pods in the mimosa stirred as a squirrel leapt from a gray limb onto a telephone wire. "Maybe I could, F.X. Try this one. There's this guy who's walking around all day dying of cancer. He's dying right before everyone's eyes, but do you think anyone cares? No, sir, the only thing they care about is their twenty-nine-inch waistline and their forty-inch biceps."

F.X.'s eyebrows went up, then relaxed, then shot up again. "Say, Bobby. What— "

"Forget it. Too late now."

F.X. reached out as if he were going to touch his brother on the shoulder—but he didn't; the arm just stayed out in the air for a moment like a Greek statue's. "I didn't know," he said solemnly. "I mean, well, hey, look, I dusted in the living room. Did you notice? You had some magazines laying around and all. I straightened them up."

"Thanks."

"Listen, why don't you go lie down, man? I'll bring you your stuff in bed. You got a tray or something?"

Mr. Pickens sighed. "I told you, it's too late. I'm okay now." He went on to explain about the nurse's phone call and the mix-up at the lab. F.X. seemed confused at first and had to have some parts repeated. Then he told Mr. Pickens he ought to sue.

"The doctor?" Mr. Pickens said. "Wasn't his fault. Besides, he's in my men's Bible study group at the Jubilee Baptist Church."

"How about the lab?" Smoke escaped as F.X. took off the frying pan lid to turn the patties. He poured a little Jack Daniel's on them—for flavoring, he explained to his brother. Mr. Pickens wondered why he had never thought of that, and finished his fourth, very stiff drink.

"The lab?" Mr. Pickens said. The word meant nothing to him for a moment. "Oh. Well, what for? I mean, nothing happened."

"What about mental incapacity? Hell, son, they shouldn't be able to get away with things like that. Tell them you had to miss work because you were so upset. Anguish—that's the word I was looking for. Mental anguish."

"I'm not sure I felt anguish." He held out his glass. "How about some of that J.D.?"

"This shit's not good for you," F.X. said, complying. "You ought to watch it."

"Anguish," Mr. Pickens said, sipping the bourbon neat. It tasted watery. "I guess what I mainly felt was, you know, unreal, like everything was a dream. Can't sue someone for making you feel unreal. And plus, the doctor never said for sure I was dying. He actually didn't say anything except that it was serious, real serious. The dying part I got from the library. I went there and looked up melamoma . . . melamo . . . whatever, in the health encyclopedia."

F.X. spooned the mashed potatoes onto a plate. "Do these look right to you?" he asked, setting them in front of his brother. Mr. Pickens squinted and thought they looked sort of like mashed potatoes. F.X. went back to the stove and dished up the veal patties, which were burned on one side. "Hell, Bobby, if I can be sued for mental anguish, I don't see why—"

"You were?"

"Better believe it, three times. First there was Charlene, then Ora and Elizabeth."

Mr. Pickens remembered Charlene. She was F.X.'s first wife; he had married her when she was still a cheerleader at Ozone High. Ora Mr. Pickens never knew but had heard about. F.X. was married to her for four years. She had gone to Vassar and got small parts in soap operas in New York; when she turned thirty, she decided to start her life anew, so she quit acting, divorced F.X., and went to law school. But Elizabeth?

"Let's see," F.X. replied to his question, "Elizabeth and I got married about five years ago, no, four. She was a real estate agent in L.A., a dynamite lady. I mean, Bobby, you wouldn't believe how good-looking she was. Anyway, this producer came along, and she fell in love, and that was that. It really tore me up. But I think I'm over it now, you know."

"Gee, I'm sorry." He yawned. "Well, well."

"Ready for your grub? Here it comes."

CHAPTER

Five

The veal patty churned in Mr. Pickens's stomach; the rash on his arm looked redder than ever. He wished he hadn't drunk that J.D., not on top of all that vodka. He was sitting in the den, watching television, while F.X. showered. After using up all the hot water a still-dripping F.X. joined him. F.X. had removed Mr. Pickens's financial records and Christmas decorations from the lowboy to make room for his clothes, which he now began trying on in front of the full-length mirror he had unscrewed from the bathroom door. He seemed to be having a hard time deciding between jeans and the jeanless look but finally settled on a pair of skin-tight slacks. After putting on a plaid cowboy shirt, however, F.X. changed his mind again and got into jeans with fancy stitching on the pockets.

"Well, be seeing you," F.X. said after he finished blow-drying his hair with a hand-held dryer that made the TV picture go fuzzy. Mr. Pickens noticed that his brother's hair was so black it looked almost blue.

"You going out?"

"I thought I told you. I got a date tonight."

"Oh." Mr. Pickens tried hard to remember being told but couldn't.

"I assume it's all right to borrow the car?"

Mr. Pickens shrugged. "Well, you know, F.X., I was planning on maybe going out myself."

F.X. twirled the keys on his index finger. "Why didn't you tell me, son? Well, who's the lucky chick—that girl you took out last night? She your girl friend?"

Mr. Pickens nodded yes, even though Burma wasn't his girl friend, even though at present he really didn't have a steady girl friend at all. This was an embarrassing fact about himself that he planned on remedying soon, maybe when inventory was over at the store and he wasn't so tired in the evenings.

"So what's her name?" F.X. asked, smiling aggressively.

Mr. Pickens sighed. He supposed he might as well let F.X. have the car tonight. Mr. Pickens could do without going to Baskin-Robbins, which was what he really wanted the car for. "I didn't know you knew anyone in Tula Springs," Mr. Pickens said dully.

"Just met her today. Look, can I have the car or not?"

Although he was going to give in eventually, Mr. Pickens

didn't want to make it too easy for him. F.X. shouldn't just *assume* he could use his car. "What's her name?"

"Toinette, Toinette something. You know her, right? Works at Sonny Boy."

"Oh." He gave a tight smile. "Yeah, I know her. How did you meet her?"

"Well, like I said, I was nosing around Sonny Boy this noon looking for you. She was the girl that came up and told me you were out to lunch. That's just what she said, 'Mr. Pickens is out to lunch,' and I said, 'You're telling me,' and she laughed and beamed out a few vibes and that was that. I got me a date."

Mr. Pickens shifted in the easy chair. "F.X., you know Toinette's much younger than she looks. She's only eighteen."

"So?"

"You're old enough to be her father. And besides, does this seem like the time to be going out on dates? There's more important things to think about, wouldn't you say? What about a job? You haven't said a word about your plans."

"Son, think. Two years now I've been cooped up without a lady. I got to get myself laid fast or I'll forget how."

The mole scar on Mr. Pickens's back began to itch; he hunched his shoulders and fidgeted.

"Hey, man," F.X. said, "tell me you understand. Tell me I've been wrong about you all these years. Tell me you're human."

"Okay, I'm human," Mr. Pickens said a little hotly. "I'm human, so I need the car tonight. I got urges too, you know."

The keys sailed over Mr. Pickens's head and clattered onto the top of the TV set. Mr. Pickens let them lie there until he heard F.X. opening the refrigerator in the other room. Then he picked them up and pocketed them.

He sat for a while mulling over the incident. It was stupid

to feel guilty. After all, it was *his* car; he could do whatever he wanted with it. If he felt like driving up and down Flat Avenue all night backward, that was *his* business. Furthermore, he was doing F.X. a favor. The last thing F.X. needed now, when he was trying to get back on his feet, was to get mixed up with someone like Toinette Quaid. If getting laid was the issue, there were plenty of ladies around for that, pros who wouldn't tangle up your life with a lot of ifs, ands, and buts. Mr. Pickens considered introducing F.X. to Miss Mina, who lived a few miles out on the Old Jefferson Davis Highway. She was attractive, clean, personable, and could even do your income tax for you, if you wanted. It was a sideline of hers. Mr. Pickens liked her but didn't pay her many visits because the smell of creosote from the plant next door made him queasy.

Mr. Pickens cranked down the footrest on the easy chair and stood up. He found F.X. in the kitchen reading the Tula Springs *Herald*.

"Hi," Mr. Pickens said, standing in the archway.

"What's up, Bobby boy?"

F.X. looked pretty friendly, as if he had forgotten the whole thing. Maybe it wasn't necessary to tell him about Miss Mina after all. Of course Mr. Pickens was aware that psychologists had discovered that the Baptists were wrong about sex, that it could be very unhealthy to repress nature. And he had seen a talk show once where a whore said that prostitution was going to be made legal within the next ten years. But he still couldn't help feeling ashamed of Miss Mina, and when it came right down to it, he'd rather no one on earth ever found out about him and her. So he walked past F.X. to the refrigerator, took out an apple he didn't want, and after saying something about the weather to F.X. went back to the den.

Sitting in the easy chair, he decided he'd go out in a few

minutes and get some ice cream, maybe see a movie over at the mall in Mississippi. It was a shame he was forced to go out on such a cold night. He would really like to just stay put and take a little snooze.

The chimes woke Mr. Pickens from his nap. He looked at his watch and saw he had been dozing for half an hour. "I'll get it," he called out, but before he could get up, F.X. was already at the door. Mr. Pickens stood up, hoping it wasn't Burma.

It wasn't Burma; it was Toinette. "I'm froze," she said to Mr. Pickens as she came in. He was standing in the doorway to the den.

"Your belt," F.X. said to him as he took Toinette's silver shawl. Mr. Pickens looked down and remembered he had unbuckled his belt after dinner; he turned his back and did it up.

F.X. hung the shawl in the hall closet. "What happened to your date?" he asked his brother.

"Mr. Pickens, could you show me your house?" Toinette asked. Her collarbone stood out sharply beneath her goose-bumped freckled skin and made her look frail, brittle, less willowy. "I've always wanted to know what the inside looked like."

F.X. draped his arm around his brother's neck. "I'll show you, Toin. Bobby's got to get going."

"But I thought Mr. Pickens was going to be here with us." Her long red-nailed toes, crammed inside open-toed spikes, curled and uncurled. "Mama would kill me if she found out. I told her Mr. Pickens would be here. You said, F.A."

"X. F.X. But you see, I forgot Bobby had a date."

"He does?" Her green eyes widened with interest.

"Well, actually . . ." Mr. Pickens began.

"Who with?" she demanded of F.X.

"He won't tell me her name. But they're hot and heavy, you better believe."

"Well, actually . . ." Mr. Pickens attempted again. He should have known his brother wasn't going to be easily discouraged; F.X. had probably called Toinette while he was napping.

"Looks deceive," F.X. went on, keeping his arm around his brother's neck. "Underneath this baby face there's a real tiger. Couldn't get enough of her last night, so he has to go back for more."

"Last night? He was with me last night." Toinette's lower lip went out. "Now, listen up, F.X., I'm not staying here alone with you. Not on a first date."

"So you and Bobby went out last night?" F.X. said, giving his brother's neck a sharp hug.

"And Burma. She's my girl friend." She went up on tiptoes and peered over Mr. Pickens's head into the den. "That's a cute lamp, that driftwood. I nearly bought one once in Fort Walton Beach. That's where Mama and me go every summer."

"Burma—is that your girl friend's name?" F.X. asked Mr. Pickens.

"No, Burma's not his girl friend," Toinette said, gazing now over her shoulder at the living room. "Burma's engaged to be married to this boy from Lucy, Mississippi, up near Vicksburg."

Engaged? Mr. Pickens was offended by this news. "F.X.," he said, trying to twist his head out of the hug that was turning his face red.

Toinette glanced at them and sniffed. "When you two are quit rasslin', I'd appreciate a Tab cola."

After extricating himself Mr. Pickens went to his bedroom and combed his mussed-up hair back into place. For good measure he stiffened the strands with hair spray so they'd stay put over the bald area. His car coat wasn't in the closet or the bathroom, so he wandered into the den and then into the kitchen looking for it. He opened the refrigerator and stared a moment, then, remembering what he was looking for, shut it and returned to the den. There it was, right before his eyes, sitting on top of the TV. He put the coat on.

"Mr. Pickens, you're not leaving, are you?" Toinette called out from the love seat when he opened the front door. F.X. was lounging against the mantel, waiting for her to finish her Tab.

"Good-bye," Mr. Pickens said.

"Mr. Pickens, wait. You got to promise not to tell my mama. Swear?"

"No, ma'am, I won't swear. As a general policy I like to tell the truth. I realize this policy must sound weird to some people, but I guess I'm just a pretty weird guy."

"Oh, shoot," Toinette said as the door shut behind him.

CHAPTER

Six

Mr. Pickens thought the day would never end. He hadn't been in the Sonny Boy Bargain Store more than five minutes before Mr. Randy, the manager, had a fit about the Roach Motels. Mr. Pickens had signed the receipt for the shipment, but Mr. Randy couldn't find them. A few inches shorter than Mr. Pickens, Mr. Randy weighed nearly twice as much. He was an expert at sniffing out trouble, which he found lurking in the most unlikely places. Last month, for instance, while supervising a general cage-cleaning in the pet department, Mr.

Randy was bitten by a gerbil. Mr. Pickens told Mr. Randy not to get excited about the Roach Motels. He promised to find them.

"I want a guarantee on that," Mr. Randy said, hitching up his lime-green pants.

Mr. Pickens eventually found the motels in the toy department next to the play eye shadow and edible lip gloss. Mr. Randy wanted to know what roaches had to do with eye shadow, and Mr. Pickens said it wasn't him that put the motels there. But he could tell that Mr. Randy didn't believe him.

During most of the day Mr. Pickens managed to avoid Toinette at the candy counter in the front of the store. He figured she must know everything by now—that F.X. wasn't his uncle, maybe even that F.X. was an ex-con. After going to a movie last night at the mall, then driving around by himself for almost an hour, Mr. Pickens had returned home and found F.X. alone. F.X. had tried to seem happy, but Mr. Pickens sensed something was wrong. When he started asking questions, though, hoping to get more details about the evening, F.X. got annoyed and went to bed. Then this morning, when Mr. Pickens got to work, Toinette blushed when he said good morning to her. He blushed back and disappeared into his office.

Just before closing, Mr. Randy summoned Mr. Pickens and asked him if he had noticed anything unusual going on at the candy counter today. Mr. Pickens lied and said he hadn't. He knew, of course, that Toinette had been sitting on a stool most of the day, a wheeled stool that allowed her to scoop candy and nuts into the white bags without standing up.

"I want you to confiscate that stool," Mr. Randy said after giving Mr. Pickens a good dressing down. Mr. Pickens was supposed to keep an eye on personnel so that Mr. Randy could tend to more important matters. "And furthermore," Mr. Randy said, tapping the plastic ID badge pinned to Mr. Pickens's lapel (Mr. R. Pickens, Asst. Man.), "you're going to dock that gal half a day's pay."

"Couldn't I just give a warning this time?"

"Half a day."

Mr. Pickens was firm with Toinette, but Toinette was firm right back. She said the stool was just sitting out there in the storeroom collecting dust. Why shouldn't she give it some use? Mr. Pickens said that as far as he was concerned, she could. But Mr. Randy said no, and there was nothing they could do about it. As Mr. Pickens rolled the stool away, he decided that he'd wait until tomorrow to tell her about getting docked.

When Mr. Pickens got home that evening, he was so tired that he dozed off in the bathtub. F.X. wasn't home—Mr. Pickens didn't know where he was—so he ate supper in the den in front of the TV. After five minutes of *The Brady Bunch* he switched to *The Three Stooges* and finished his Salisbury steak. When the door chimes rang, he turned the channel to local news before seeing who it was.

A large, buxom woman stood on the front porch. "Mr. Pickens?" she asked in a gravelly, almost mannish voice, then started coughing into her fist.

"Yes?" he said after she recovered.

"Mrs. Quaid, Marie Antoinette's mother. Mind if I come in?"

Breathing deeply to still the vague anxiety she aroused in him, Mr. Pickens ushered her into the living room, where she sat down in a tightly stuffed armchair. "Which one are you, now?" she said, offering him a cigarette from the pack of Camels she drew out of her pocket; he shook his head. "You F.X. or the nephew?"

"Actually, Mrs. Quaid, F.X. is my brother, half brother. Toinette must have got things a little confused."

"Wouldn't be the first time," she said, unbuttoning her pea jacket. She had on a white uniform, something like a nurse's, and rubber-soled orthopedic shoes that had squeaked loudly when she walked over the pine floor. Something about her stirred a memory in Mr. Pickens, very dimly, though.

"F.X. around? I'd like to talk with him too, if I could."

"No, ma'am, he's gone."

She adjusted her hairnet, which had left a red crease across her forehead. An unlit cigarette dangled from her mouth as she said, "Mr. Pickens, Marie Antoinette came home very upset last night. I'd like to know what happened."

"You and me both, Miss Quaid."

She sucked on the unlit cigarette, keeping her gray eyes focused on him. "What's that supposed to mean?"

"I tried to find out myself."

"You were here, though."

"No, Miss Quaid. I wasn't."

She tapped a large mole near her nose. "Toinette told me you would chaperone. It's the only reason I let her come. I thought I could trust you, Mr. Pickens, seeing as how you work with her and all."

"No one told *me* I was supposed to chaperone. I happened to have had an important engagement last night." Mr. Pickens drew himself up erect on the plastic-covered love seat, which, in the dimly lit room, had the color of a not-quite-ripe tomato.

"I see," Mrs. Quaid said, and stared vacantly at a pot of elephant ears near the mantel. Then she began rummaging in her purse. "This brother of yours, how old is he?"

"Around forty."

She shook her head. "And that girl swore up and down he was young, in his twenties or something. Kept on saying you had a mixed-up family, that's how come the uncle was so young." A dainty gold lighter came out of her purse; she flicked it but didn't put the flame to the cigarette. "What's he do, Mr. Pickens?"

Mr. Pickens shrugged.

The flame went out, and Mrs. Quaid set the lighter down on the end table and looked at it. "Maybe you think I'm being nosy." She sighed and crossed her swollen ankles. "I know I shouldn't meddle, but you see, Toinette's dad is away a lot, and I'm the one left holding the ball. He's down at Morgan City, works on the rigs six weeks at a time."

"Frankly, Miss Quaid, I don't think you meddle enough. If I were you, I'd forbid Toinette to ever see F.X. again. Not only is he old and out of a job, but he's been married three times already. And furthermore . . ." Mr. Pickens stopped himself. He had given her enough reasons already.

"Hon, you think it's that easy? You think I can just say no to that girl once she sets her mind on something? Lord, then you don't know Toinette." She started coughing again. When she stopped, she reached for the lighter and lit her cigarette. She drew deeply on it and closed her eyes with relief.

"A firm hand never hurt anyone," Mr. Pickens said. He crossed his legs and waved away some smoke. "You know, Miss Quaid, you look awfully familiar."

She picked up a *Reader's Digest* and tried to fan the smoke in a different direction, away from Mr. Pickens. "It's funny, you're not anything like I thought you'd be."

"What do you mean?"

"Toinette's always talking about you, you know. I pictured someone much . . . littler."

"Littler?"

"Let me open this window," she said, halfway rising.

"It's all right. The smoke doesn't bother me." Paws clicked on the porch outside the window; it was the Gaglionis' dog from down the street making his nightly inspection. "I'm curious, Miss Quaid, what does your daughter say about me?" He smiled to encourage her.

"Nothing. Just a bunch of nonsense." She blew a smoke ring and watched it drift toward the mantel. "She's full of beans."

"No, really, I'm always interested in what my coworkers have to say." He smiled again earnestly.

Mrs. Quaid regarded him for a moment. "You are, huh? Well, then, for one thing, she says you stole her watch."

The earnest smile remained on his face. "I'm afraid I don't understand," he said, his eyes glazing over.

"Marie Antoinette gets notions. It's nothing to worry about. She's young and stupid, still doesn't know the first thing about life."

"But . . ." His tongue strayed out to moisten his lips.

"I told her she better stop taking the darn watch off. Ever since she overheard someone say in the beauty college that gold gives you cancer, she's been afraid to keep it on too long at a time. Did you ever hear such nonsense? I warned her she was going to lose it someday. She's got only herself to blame." Mrs. Quaid squinted as smoke rose to her eyes. "And I warned her too. I said, 'Darling, don't you dare go pointing fingers till you got proof. That's against the law. You could lose your job and maybe worse.'" She stubbed out her cigarette in a plastic ashtray; it was only half smoked. "But that's not the only thing she says about you. She says nice things too."

"Oh?" he said faintly.

She smiled, revealing a gold incisor. "Says you look funny at her—thinks you been bit by the love bug. Oh, Mr. Pickens, hon, don't look so upset." She patted his hand. "Toinette thinks everyone and everything's in love with her, including the pet turtle she let starve to death."

"I'm not upset." The plastic on the love seat crinkled as he changed positions. "I'm amazed, simply amazed."

"You got to understand," she said, picking up the half-smoked cigarette in the ashtray and putting it in her mouth. "Toinette likes drama. She's not happy 'less she's got drama all around her. When I come home at night after trying to feed two hundred of my little chickens, I don't want drama. No, ma'am, I want peace, not drama."

"You work at the hatcheries?"

"Chickens is just what I call my kids. I'm the head dietician at Tula Springs High."

He knew now why she looked so familiar. Without too much effort—taking away some of the wrinkles, a little flesh from the cheeks, the gray in her hair—he saw her standing behind the lunchroom counter when he was in high school. It was hard to believe that anyone could survive a job like that for so long; she must have been at it for more than thirty years.

"Cat got your tongue?"

"Pardon?" He had been daydreaming.

"I asked if you're married."

Mr. Pickens hesitated; it was really none of her business. "Not presently."

"Didn't think so. Mr. Randy, though, that's another story. He's married, isn't he?"

Mr. Pickens nodded.

"Uh-huh, I thought so." She finally lit her cigarette. "Just goes to show you what sort of place that is, Sonny Boy. A married man."

"I'm afraid I don't follow."

"I told Toinette she ought to go on to college. I asked her what sort of folk she wants to associate with—the type you find at St. Jude or the type you find in a place like Sonny Boy. She claims it don't make any difference to her—they're both the same as far as she's concerned. 'Okay, Miss Know-It-All,' I say to her. 'You go work at Sonny Boy and you'll find out who's right.' And I'll be hung if it weren't but a day or two later she gets propositioned by that Mr. Randy. He promised that if she gave him a little sugar, he'd make her assistant manager."

Mrs. Quaid eyed her host to make sure he was getting the full effect of the story. Satisfied by his look that he was, she continued in her harsh, raspy voice: "When I heard that, I said, 'Okay, sister, that's it.' But she put up a big fuss and said how ugly and fat Mr. Randy was and how there was no danger at all. But I didn't trust Toinette. I had to take a good look for myself. So one day I come down to Sonny Boy pretending to be your normal, everyday customer. See, I never really shop there. I go to the mall, where they take credit cards. Anyway, I pretend I'm looking for this special knife sharpener—it's just something I made up off the top of my head. So when the clerk can't find it, I ask to see the manager." She smiled and slapped some ash off her uniform. "You better believe, hon, when that ole Mr. Randy comes waddling out of his office, I know right then and there I don't have to worry about my Toinette no more. She'd have to be plum nuts to want to be assistant manager."

While Mr. Pickens sat there, mute, his rash itching fiercely, Mrs. Quaid sucked the Camel down until it almost burned her fingers. Then, stubbing it out, she said she better run. She had to get to the shoe repair shop before it closed.

"You tell that F.X. he better not hurt my baby," she said at the door, then left.

CHAPTER

Seven

"You'll be boiled, you'll be strangled, you'll be boiled, and I shall skin you, I'll skin you, I'll skin you, I'll behead, then I'll hang you to a pole, I then will pin you, you'll be boiled, you'll be strangled, you'll be boiled, and I shall skin you." Decked out in baggy gold pants, pointed shoes, and a paisley turban, the bass finished his aria on a triumphant note and strode offstage to polite, scattered applause, which awakened Mr. Pickens. The opera was being performed at Black Angus Coliseum, the large, domed wooden hall where St. Jude State College hosted livestock exhibitions, rodeos, and graduation exercises for local high schools. Normally St. Jude's music department held its concerts in the student union, but the light board in the student-union auditorium had caught fire the previous week, so they were forced to move the whole production to the coliseum.

Mr. Pickens had come by himself. He wore his best blue-checked suit with the reversible silk vest, and a brand-new tie that he had bought at Fraternity Row, the most expensive men's shop in the mall over in Mississippi. When the lights came up at intermission, he stood up gratefully from the hard metal folding chair and looked about him at the other members of the opening night audience. Beside him was a lady in a mink stole, the kind that had the heads left on it. As Mr. Pickens brushed against the fur to get by her, his eyes met the eyes of a mink—small, black, vicious beads that glared at him in outrage.

A week had passed since Mrs. Quaid's visit, and a strange, depressing week it had been. With no warning the weather had changed, turning the crisp November air into a rank soup that smelled of hearty weeds, yellowing lawns, and mutts on the loose. F.X. used the air-conditioner at night to drown out the tree frogs in the chinaberry, as well as the teenagers, who, now that it was warm, congregated in greater numbers at Dr. Henry's. Work for Mr. Pickens had never been so unpleasant. He could barely stand to look at Mr. Randy after what Mrs. Quaid had told him, and at the same time he found himself staring at Toinette more than was necessary. He was afraid of her—at least that's what he thought at first. F.X. still wouldn't say a word about what had happened on their date. In fact he never talked about her at all, even though Mr. Pickens suspected that he was still seeing her on the sly. Mr. Pickens worried constantly that Toinette was going to accuse him in public about the watch, and his heart beat fast and erratically whenever he had to talk to her. When he finally summoned up the courage to tell her about being docked because of the stool, though, Toinette looked more sad than angry, which wasn't like her at all. Mr. Pickens went home that evening feeling more disturbed than ever. But it wasn't until he had changed into his yard clothes and was pulling up alligator grass near the ditch in the backyard that the truth finally dawned on him: He was falling in love with Toinette.

Unlike most men, Mr. Pickens did not fall in love easily and often. In fact it was safe to say that until now he had never truly been in love with anyone. Why this was so, he didn't know. It worried him a great deal until he finally decided that most people were like him: they only *said* they were in love, when at best they simply had a big crush, which, as always, would soon wear off. But now something told him that at forty-one he was about to experience the real thing. It was a frightening thought. Deep inside he knew there would be only one woman in his life, one or none at all. Why, then, did this woman have to be someone like Toinette? He couldn't imagine a worse choice, not in a million years. She was way too young, three or four inches too tall, and what's more, he didn't really like her that much.

Astir with a muddled, half-formed love for Toinette that was growing stronger by the minute, Mr. Pickens resolved to transfer this feeling—before it was too late—to real wife material, a mature woman who was sober, industrious, intelligent, and if not beautiful, at least well groomed. That was the reason he began going out in the evenings to places he didn't want to go to—a party at his mother's old friend Mrs. Bingham's, where the youngest woman turned out to be fifty; a lecture at L.S.U. entitled "The Decline of the Nutria Industry in Louisiana" (Mrs. Bingham's great-niece gave the lecture, but Mrs. Bingham had forgotten that this great-niece was happily married, a fact Mr. Pickens discovered after sitting through the entire lecture and a long question-and-answer period afterward); and now an opera, which was pure torture. Though bored out of his mind, he was mature enough to realize that great music such as this was supposed to have a good effect on you, whether you liked it or not; so he endured it.

Mr. Pickens walked toward the west exit of the coliseum, where a concession stand was selling soft drinks and cotton candy. While standing in line he finally saw someone he recognized—his dentist from Tula Springs. Not many people from Tula Springs went to cultural events at St. Jude—except for old Mrs. Jenks, who reviewed them for the Tula Springs *Herald*, concentrating mainly on what people wore. Mr. Pickens smiled and nodded at the dentist, but he must not have seen him, because he looked away and started talking to his wife.

After buying a Dr Pepper, Mr. Pickens went and stood near the dentist. Perhaps he just didn't recognize him, Mr. Pickens thought when the dentist turned his back on him; after all, it had been a year since he had had his teeth cleaned. He worked on an opening gambit, something like, *Hi, I guess with my mouth closed you don't recognize me.* While he refined this remark the dentist and his wife were joined by a nice-looking young couple whom the wife introduced to the dentist as Jerry and Jill. Jerry and Jill, Mr. Pickens overheard, had driven from New Orleans that night because Jill's brother was one of the janissaries in the opera. Jill said the causeway was slippery tonight, and someone had skidded right in front of them. Mr. Pickens caught Jill's eye, and she smiled at him. He opened his mouth to say that he had once skidded on the causeway, but then Jerry said in a loud voice that he was enjoying the opera, but he wished it wasn't so stuffy and hot.

Mr. Pickens steeled himself. It was now or never. This would be his last chance to meet a young couple like Jerry and Jill, people who probably knew a whole batch of nice, attractive single women. "Hi," Mr. Pickens said to Jill, who smiled encouragingly at him, "I guess with my mouth closed you don't recognize me."

Jill opened her eyes a little wider; her husband put an arm around her, frowned at Mr. Pickens, and told his wife he wanted a soda. The dentist and his wife followed Jerry and Jill to the concession stand. Appalled at his stupidity, Mr. Pickens held up his mimeographed program and pretended to read it: *Belmonte . . . Curtis C. Mayhaw, IV . . . Wolfgang Amadeus . . . Act I—A garden in front of Pasha Selim's palace . . . Constanze . . .*

"Mr. Pickens!"

A familiar voice, a tug at his sleeve. He looked up and saw Burma. Her hair piled high on her head, she was wearing a complicated dress that looked something like a crinoline trimmed with lace. "Mr. Pickens, what are *you* doing here!" she cried, her eyes bright with excitement.

"Just looking at the opera," he replied more temperately; her enthusiasm was not infectious.

"I didn't know you liked music!" She squeezed his arm; then, looking over her shoulder, she caught sight of a young man standing a few feet away. "Hey, where did you go to?" she said, beckoning to him. The young man approached. He was dark, darker than F.X. even, and had a scar over his right eye that made his face look unbalanced. Burma told him to shake hands with Mr. Pickens.

"This is my fiancé," she said as they shook hands. "Emmet Orney. Emmet, this is Mr. Pickens, the man I'm always telling you about."

Emmet blushed and looked down at the sawdust on the floor. "Hey," he muttered, then pulled out a wad of tissues from his trousers and blew his nose, or tried to; it was a very dry sound.

"I been hoping you two could meet someday and be friends," Burma said, brushing some lint off Emmet's madras jacket. "Emmet's just got out of the Army. He's at St. Jude now, plays the flute."

"Clarinet," Emmet said softly.

"I mean clarinet." Burma looked hopefully at her boss, but Mr. Pickens didn't say anything. "Do you like clarinets?"

Mr. Pickens said he did.

"Maybe one night you can come over and Emmet will play for you. I don't know why I said flute," she backtracked. "You must think I'm a real ninny."

Mr. Pickens denied this. He noticed the dentist was looking at him, so he repositioned himself behind Burma.

"Are you here by yourself, Mr. Pickens? If you are, why don't you come sit over by us? There's an extra space."

Mr. Pickens smiled obscurely.

"I hope you're planning on coming to our wedding next month," she went on. "Toinette's helping me plan it. We're having a music theme for it. There's going to be notes on the cake and candy clarinets and—"

"No clarinets," Emmet said softly through clenched teeth.

Burma slapped his shoulder. "Hush, Emmet, I already told you we was having clarinets. You can't go changing your mind now." She smiled at Mr. Pickens. "Oh, and then we got one of Emmet's friends to play the piano, plus I'm checking up on some ice to see if we can get it carved to look like a note. What do you call those black notes, Emmet?"

"Quarter notes," he said, gazing at the steel rafters in the dome.

"That's right, a big ice quarter note."

Mr. Pickens managed to slip away from Burma and Emmet before they all sat down again. The dentist and his wife returned to their seats followed by old Mrs. Jenks, who had a corsage pinned to her ample bosom.

At the next intermission Burma made Emmet stand up on his chair and look over the sea of heads for Mr. Pickens. Glancing nervously over his shoulder, Mr. Pickens hurried toward the east exit and the parking lot. He would have liked to see the last act of the opera—not because he was enjoying the singing but because he thought if you were going to absorb culture, it didn't count unless you absorbed the whole thing.

The coliseum was right across the street from Lake Pontchartrain. As he drove past the oaks and palms lining the shore he was conscious of the red light of an oil derrick far out in the dark, calm waters. No matter how fast he went, the light was always there, steady and unblinking, as if he were not really moving at all, as if the breeze created by the car were a real breeze, touching not just him through the opened window but everything in its path. Yet there were no white-caps, and the palm fronds did not stir.

To get to Tula Springs he passed through Ozone with its gracious lakefront houses. There used to be a ferry here, allowing people to escape from the New Orleans heat in the summer; but when the causeway was built at Mandeville, the ferry was discontinued, and many of Ozone's houses were neglected and fell into disrepair. Ozone was now a resort town without vacationers, its beaches largely unused, the drive-in, which once did a thriving business, silent. He slowed down at the weather-beaten, sagging screen of the Ozone Lux, which faced the lake. Here he turned north, away from the lake, onto an elevated interstate that cut a straight line through a wilderness of swamp and half-dead cypress, a spillway for the Mississippi. A half hour later the landscape changed abruptly. He was in the piney woods, climbing gradually, imperceptibly away from the rich bottomland to the harsher, meager soil of Tula Springs.

CHAPTER

Eight

At Sonny Boy the next day Burma tried to give a refund to an old woman who returned a defective Secret Agent pen. The old woman had written a long letter in invisible ink to her grandson, but she said when the grandson got it and held it over a flame, no writing appeared on the paper, not a word. Mr. Randy happened to be standing in the next aisle and overheard the complaint. After Burma had promised the old woman a refund and was on her way to the cash register, Mr. Randy came over and told the old woman there were no refunds. The old woman demanded a sheet of paper, and Burma obliged by ripping one from a note pad. Then the old woman wrote something on the ruled paper and handed it to Mr. Randy. "Read that for me, Mr. Gen. Man.," she said, peering through her bifocals at his ID badge.

Mr. Randy screwed up his eyes and held the paper close to his stubby nose. "You got to hold it over a flame," he said.

"I'll get a candle," Burma volunteered.

"A *broken* candle," Mr. Randy said. A real cheapskate, he kept a special drawer in which his clerks deposited defective merchandise such as chipped statuettes, stationery that was water-stained, and broken candles. Burma, though, did not go to this drawer. Instead, when Mr. Randy's back was turned, she snitched the best candle she could find from the display bin, unwrapped it, then broke it in half. After she gave this to Mr. Randy, he ordered her to go help Toinette at the candy counter.

Burma obeyed, but she was peeved at him for not giving the poor old woman her money back. She told Toinette about the incident, and both of them started moving real slow at the candy counter, taking forever to weigh the peanuts and kisses and then making change like it was their first day on the job. Mr. Randy ordered Mr. Pickens to go straighten the girls out, so Mr. Pickens had to go over to the candy counter and warn them. That was when Burma told him the whole story of the Secret Agent pen. Mr. Pickens sympathized with her and said it wasn't fair of Mr. Randy. Burma said if he thought that, why didn't he go over and say something to Mr. Randy. She was a little grouchy today because she hadn't got to say good-bye to Mr. Pickens at the opera last night.

"Don't blame Mr. Pickens," Toinette said. "It's not his fault."

Mr. Pickens tried not to feel too good when he heard this, but when he looked in her eyes, he couldn't help it. Those green eyes, which had always seemed so cold to him, were warm enough now to melt Burma's quarter note. Burma turned her back on them and sniffed loudly.

"Burma, you owe Sonny Boy thirty-nine cents plus tax," Mr. Randy said, looming up on them from out of nowhere. Mr. Pickens sidled over to the next counter and, from a ring on his belt, chose a key that opened the glass case where wallets were displayed. He rearranged some of the wallets while listening in on Mr. Randy.

"Thirty-nine cents for what?" Burma demanded.

"This here Lucky Eagle number nine-nine-oh note pad you ripped up."

"Can I write you a check?"

"I'll deduct it Friday. And you girls stop snitching cashews," he added as he walked back toward his office.

That evening Mr. Pickens went to work in his backyard again, trying to make the area around the ditch look neater. After clearing away the alligator grass and the disreputable-looking sumac, he planned to sod the area over with St. Augustine, which his mother's friend Mrs. Bingham promised to give him. F.X. toted the alligator grass and some trash from the ditch—beer bottles, candy wrappers, a doll leg—to the front in a wheelbarrow, then returned and began peeling an orange-and-purple fungus from the trunk of the Chinese tallow tree.

"Don't do that," Mr. Pickens said, wiping the sweat from his forehead with his dirty garden gloves. "You might hurt the tree."

F.X. tossed the pulpy fungus into the ditch and sat down. "What's wrong with you?" he asked good-naturedly.

"Nothing." Mr. Pickens yanked up the roots of a scrubby sumac. "Nothing, 'cept I'm tired, tired to death, F.X."

"Take a nap."

"Not that kind of tired. I'm talking about mentally tired. Sonny Boy is getting me down. All day long it's bicker, bicker, bicker. I don't know if I can take it much longer. As a matter of fact, I've a good mind to quit."

F.X. tugged at some milkweed. "Don't quit yet, son."

"Why not?"

"I was counting on you. Remember, you said you'd loan me a few bucks for a set of weights."

"F.X."

"So what are you going to do if you quit? Jobs aren't so easy to come by these days."

"I'll find something. Starting tomorrow, I'm going to put out some feelers. Then, soon as I get a good job, I'm going to tell Zell P. Randy what he can do with his stupid Sonny Boy."

A dragonfly alighted on a rainbow of oil in the ditch water. When F.X. tried to bomb the insect with a stone, water splashed on his brother.

"Thanks, F.X."

F.X. smothered a laugh. "Sorry."

"Sorry."

"Hey, man, what's eating you? It's just a little water."

Mr. Pickens yanked at a clump of grass. "Sonny Boy isn't the only thing I'm tired of."

"What's that supposed to mean?"

"I'm not made out of money, F.X. Did you ever stop to think about that?"

"Who bought the hamburgers last night?"

"Great. You buy one dinner. I mean, what do you think this

is, some sort of resort? You're practically forty, yet all you do
all day is nothing—nothing but sneak around with teenagers."

"Teenagers?"

"You know who I mean. That girl."

F.X. looked puzzled. "What girl? Oh, not Tonie Whatcha-
madig?"

Mr. Pickens could see why his brother was not a success; he
was a terrible actor. "Yeah, Toinette. I know you've been seeing her."

"You got to be kidding." F.X. tugged on the Chinese tallow,
a frail sapling. "I can do better than that. Besides, she's just
a kid."

"Don't," Mr. Pickens cautioned; F.X. was bending back the
slender trunk to an alarming angle. "You mean you're really
not seeing her?"

"I told you, Bobby," he said testily. The sapling whipped
upright as he released it.

"You're really seeing Mike in Ozone—at night? I don't get
it. Why can't he see you during the day?"

"Look, I don't argue with parole officers. If he wants to see
me at night, I see him at night."

Mollified but still not totally convinced that F.X. was telling
the truth, Mr. Pickens tossed some weeds into the wheelbarrow.

"This is a hard time for me, Bobby, you got to understand.
I can't just go barreling into the first job that comes along.
I got a career to think about." A mud dauber dangled its legs
over F.X.'s head. Mr. Pickens watched it hover there, as if it
were trying to make up its mind whether F.X. was worth
stinging. The insect flew off lazily. "Being an actor isn't easy.
You got to know yourself inside out; you got to be in tune
with yourself. That's what I'm working at now, getting in touch
with myself again. Angola really screwed me up something
awful, you can't imagine. I got all this hostility I can't deal

with. My head's just not together." He leaned over and picked a dandelion and put it in the wheelbarrow. "In any case, I know it's hard on you. I appreciate what you're doing for me. As a matter of fact, I've been thinking hard about money. Just today I talked to someone at the hatcheries."

"About a job?" Mr. Pickens asked.

"Not exactly. See, I was thinking of maybe buying some chickens. If we raised our own eggs and meat, our food bill would be next to nothing. Then we could have a garden and—"

"Chickens? What do you know about chickens?"

"The man said he'd give me a pamphlet that would explain everything."

"F.X., we can't raise chickens here."

"Why not? You majored in farming, didn't you, at college? Let's put it to use, son. They say pigs are easy too, real economical. I saw a program on TV this morning that said—"

"Stop. F.X., look—" Mr. Pickens gestured toward Dr. Henry's, then Mrs. Wedge's house on the other side of the yard, and finally to the Hollywood Apartments across the ditch. "This is a *town* we're living in."

"So?"

"There's zoning laws."

"Zoning, schmoning." F.X. yawned, then peered skeptically at the sunset, a bronze and murky purple the color of a bruise.

Down the steps of the Hollywood Apartments came a young woman who began hanging laundry on the clothesline. The sunset was right behind her, melting away her edges, blurring her motions.

"Here it is almost dark, and she's putting out clothes," Mr. Pickens said, laying a sumac in the wheelbarrow. "I swear."

"You sound like Dad."

"What?"

"Always criticizing. Me, I believe if you don't have something good to say, you shouldn't say anything."

Mr. Pickens watched his brother go back to the small frame house, which needed a good coat of paint and new awnings. He didn't say anything.

CHAPTER

Nine

When Mr. Pickens went to work the next day, he was fired. Mr. Randy told him he was sorry to do it, but surely Mr. Pickens understood that the economy was in trouble. Everybody in the whole United States was cutting back. Mr. Pickens said he didn't think this was a good enough reason, so Mr. Randy gave him a better one. He said he didn't think Mr. Pickens was doing a very good job handling personnel. He was too easy on people, let them get away with murder.

Mr. Pickens brooded all morning about the injustice. At noon he couldn't stand it any longer. He told Mr. Randy he wasn't going to stay the whole day; he was taking his things out of his desk right now and leaving for good. If Mr. Randy wanted to dock him for the half day, that was fine with him. Mr. Randy said he wouldn't.

Nearly blind with anger, Mr. Pickens missed the turn off Flat Avenue that he wanted, and had to U-turn and circle back and make it again. He drove past the Catholic church and the little upholstery shop next to it, past the discount bakery shop where you could get slightly stale goods at half-price (his anger abated slightly when he saw that English muffins, his favorite, were on sale this week), and after a curve pulled up in front of the bicycle racks at the high school.

In the annex a workman white with plaster told him to go out back. They were using a tent there until they were through renovating the lunchroom.

Mr. Pickens went behind the annex. Beside a huge seven-hundred-and-fifty-year-old live oak named Miss Livvy (Miss Livvy was a charter member of the Aurelia Society, which accepted only the very oldest certified live oaks in the state) was a canvas tent that the school board used for exhibitions at the parish fair. There were about fifty students in line, and one of them, a pretty girl with carrot-orange hair, kicked him on the anklebone when he tried to get ahead.

"I'm not eating," Mr. Pickens yelled at the weary blue-haired teacher who was punching tickets at the entrance. "I must see Mrs. Quaid."

"Mizrus who?" She cupped a hand to her ear. "DaWannette Smith, get that finger out of your nose."

"Quaid, Quaid."

"Let me see your ticket."

A scream came from the end of the line. The old teacher, whose polka-dot dress hung unevenly about her calves, shoved past Mr. Pickens to investigate. He saw her rap a burly teen-ager on the head with her metal puncher; then he crammed himself inside the tent.

The smell carried him right back to 1957—creamed chipped beef, apple brown Betty. Mrs. Quaid was behind the stainless-steel counter, dishing out pale lima beans. When she saw him, she stopped for a moment, surprised, and just stood there.

"I got to talk to you," Mr. Pickens said, moving behind the counter.

"Pickens, what are you doing here?" she asked, looking harassed. The hairnet she was wearing had a piece of tissue clinging to it. "Next," she called out, anxious to keep the line moving.

"Miss Quaid, I've been fired."

"What? Hey, no seconds yet," she said as a boy held out his plate. "Wait till everyone's been served, hon." The boy slouched back to the crowded rows of benches, a pat of butter clinging to his behind. Over by the milk cooler someone dropped a plate, which cracked against one of Miss Livvy's roots. The worker next to Mrs. Quaid put down her soup ladle and went to pick up the pieces.

"Here, till she comes back," Mrs. Quaid said, handing Mr. Pickens the ladle.

"Mr. Randy fired me," he said, dipping into the cream of asparagus soup.

"I'm sorry, Pickens, but what do you want me to do about it?" She glanced worriedly at the garbage cans into which leftovers were scraped.

"Don't you understand? I was the assistant manager. Now guess who's going to be made assistant manager?"

Mrs. Quaid dug her spoon into the mushy beans. "No, can't be."

"Yes, ma'am, your daughter, Toinette. Why the hell do you think I got fired? I've been there seven years—never been late once, had a perfect record, never did a thing wrong, not a thing."

"But Mr. Randy, he's so ugly. My little baby just couldn't have . . ." Her face went dark and seemed to shrivel up. "Trash, just plain trash," she muttered. Then louder she said, "Pickens, you mean to tell me that—"

"I'm telling you the *truth*," he said, his face glowing with righteousness.

"I don't want the truth, Pickens—not from you. Just give me the facts."

Stung, Mr. Pickens recited what had happened to him at Sonny Boy that morning, leaving out the part where he was criticized for not handling personnel very well. He also added something that he thought he remembered now: Toinette and Mr. Randy *had* exchanged some very meaningful looks at the candy counter this morning, real deep looks.

"There's your facts, ma'am," he concluded while ladling soup onto the carrot-haired girl's chipped beef. She was gazing into her compact as she went down the line and didn't notice.

The ticket puncher walked over to Mrs. Quaid and said loud enough for Mr. Pickens to hear, "Lou, who's that?"

"No one," Mrs. Quaid replied, taking the ladle away from him.

"Can't have unauthorized personnel behind the counter," she said, smoothing out her polka-dot dress. "Against regulations."

"You better go," Mrs. Quaid told him.

Mr. Pickens left; he felt much better.

CHAPTER

Ten

Toinette had her head buried under his pillow, her long bronze-red hair peeking out at the edges. Mr. Pickens stood over her, wondering if it would help if he covered her with the afghan. But when she felt the blanket against her leg, she pulled it off and sat up. "Leave me alone," she said. Mascara had run down her cheeks, and the pillow had made a dent in her hairdo, but even so Mr. Pickens thought she looked lovely.

"Don't be . . ." Mr. Pickens began, meaning to say, *Don't be mad at me*. But his jaw ached something fierce. A half hour earlier, just after putting his fist through the front window, F.X. had aimed a punch at Toinette, which Mr. Pickens, who was reaching for a Kleenex, had accidentally intercepted. The pain was still fresh, and the jaw seemed to be swelling.

"I hate you," Toinette said. "I hate everybody."

Mr. Pickens sat down on the edge of the bed. He really couldn't blame her for hating everybody, especially him. Far from being promoted to assistant manager—as he had fully expected she would be—Toinette had been fired today along with Mr. Pickens. Alarmed by Mr. Pickens's report, though, Mrs. Quaid had laid into Toinette, accusing her of the worst before Toinette had had a chance to tell her she had been fired too. Toinette was so mad at her mother for thinking such a thing was possible between her and Mr. Randy that she had decided to run away from home.

Vanity bag in hand—that was all she had time to pack while her mother begged for forgiveness—Toinette had shown up at 517 Sweetgum Street to give Mr. Pickens a piece of her mind. "He accused me of sleeping with Mr. Randy," she said to F.X., who was home then. When he heard she had been fired, Mr. Pickens apologized profusely and asked if there was anything he could do to make up for it. Yes, she replied. You can give me money for a motel. Toinette wanted to stay with Burma and her mother, but Emmet was using the spare bedroom.

Mr. Pickens told Toinette she was welcome to stay with them. F.X. could move out of the den, and she could use the fold-out sofa. She was about to say yes, when F.X. said no. Mr. Pickens asked what was wrong with her staying for a few days, but F.X. just shook his head and said no.

"It's my house," Mr. Pickens said, and that's when F.X. put his fist through the front window. As blood dripped all over the pine floor and onto the porcelain blue jay perched next to the curtains, Toinette sobbed convulsively. Reaching across her for a Kleenex, Mr. Pickens heard F.X. shout "Slut!" and then felt F.X.'s fist crack against his jaw. F.X. left the house, leaving a trail of dark drops behind him.

"I'm sorry," Mr. Pickens said, stiff-jawed.

Toinette dabbed at her eyes with his handkerchief. "I bet I'm a mess." She got up and went into the bathroom. Mr. Pickens heard the water run.

"I just hope you're satisfied, Bobby Pickens," she said, emerging from the bathroom with the mascara repaired. "You've done a pretty good job today. Broke up me and my mama, lost me my job—"

"I didn't . . ." He wanted to say he had nothing to do with her getting fired.

"What?"

Mr. Pickens pointed to his jaw.

"You can't talk? Well, hallelujah, brother."

She reached in her vanity bag for a hairbrush, then worked the brush slowly through the luxurious mass of bronze-red hair. He looked away; he could not gaze at that hair without wanting to touch it, with his hands, with his cheeks—so he looked away. There was a worse ache inside him than the ache in his jaw. It was discovering that F.X. really did care about her. Why else would he have put his fist through the window and then called her a slut?

"Do you love him?" he asked, clenching his fists.

"What? I can't understand what you're saying."

Painful as it was, he tried again. But the phone rang, interrupting him in mid-question. He stood up to answer it.

"Sit," Toinette said, her green eyes flashing anger again. "It's my mother."

"But—"

"But nothing. I plan to teach that woman a good lesson. Now sit back down or you'll feel this brush on your jaw."

Mr. Pickens sat down.

"Quit looking at me like that," she said, her voice less harsh now.

He went red in the face, which seemed to please her.

"Does it hurt?" she asked. She put down the brush and walked over to the bed. Her hand touched his jaw, probed it gently, and he was healed. At least, that's what it seemed like. Never had he felt such peace, such a sweet peace. But when she walked back to the chest of drawers, the ache returned, deeper and fiercer than ever.

"I guess since I can't stay here, I'll need some money then."

He gave her forty dollars, which was all the cash he had in the house. She was going to spend the night in Ozone at the Pontchartrain Courts. Burma had already been there once and said they had vibrating beds; Toinette decided she wanted to know what a vibrating bed felt like too. Plus, she told him, she wanted to be able to stay up as late as she felt like, watching TV. At home her mother was always busting into the living room and telling her to go to bed.

"And one more thing," she said as he walked out onto the porch with her. Starlings bustled about in the front yard, their dark wings luminous with sudden flashes of color—hard mineral hues. "Don't you dare tell Mama where I am. I want her to stew a little tonight, hear?"

"Well . . ."

"Hear?"

He nodded. Her high wooden platform shoes clomped down the sidewalk that divided the front yard in two. The starlings exploded into the air; then, once she had got into her Dart, they settled down again to poke around the green and yellow grass.

Back inside the house, Mr. Pickens went straight to the telephone and dialed Mrs. Quaid. Although it cost him considerable pain because of his jaw, he managed to tell her not to worry about her daughter. She was at the Pontchartrain Courts and in the morning, after giving everyone a good scare, she would come home again. No, he assured her as Mrs. Quaid flared up, F.X. wasn't with her. Toinette would be alone. Good, Mrs. Quaid said. She would go fetch her home then. It took him ten minutes to convince her that she should leave well enough alone. Toinette would only run away again if she didn't think she had taught her mother a lesson.

F.X. returned home around nine o'clock that evening. When he heard the car door slam, Mr. Pickens, who had been dozing on the love seat, jerked awake and picked up the piece of cardboard lying on the floor. He had already taken the glass out of the broken pane and measured and cut the cardboard. But he wanted to make sure F.X. saw him tape the cardboard up, hoping this would prompt F.X. to offer to pay for a new pane.

F.X. strode into the kitchen, his right hand bandaged in an expert way; he must have been to a doctor. A beer can popped open.

"So where is she?" F.X. asked, coming into the living room.

Mr. Pickens—on his knees, taping—just shrugged. He moved the porcelain blue jay, which still had blood on its wings, out of the way.

"Did she go home?"

Mr. Pickens pointed to his jaw.

"Look, I'm sorry about that." He went to the mantel, picked up a pewter candle snuffer, and tapped out a nervous rhythm with it. "Want a beer?"

Mr. Pickens shook his head. The cardboard was up. It was

amazing what one piece of cardboard could do, Mr. Pickens thought as he gauged its effect. What had been tacky in the room—his mother's love seat, for instance—now became downright seedy. Well, he hoped F.X. was satisfied.

Going to the end table, where the photo album was kept, Mr. Pickens found a pencil and paper. Using the album as a support on his lap, he wrote, *I'm in too much pain to talk. Why do you want to know where she is?*

"I just wanted to apologize for you," F.X. said, crumbling up the note after he had read it.

For me! Mr. Pickens scribbled. *I didn't call her a slut!*

"I wasn't calling *her* a slut," he replied, tossing the second note into the fireplace, where a wilted fern sat. "I meant you, for snitching on her."

You tried to punch her. Mr. Pickens handed him the note, then flexed his hand, which was cramping.

"I punched you, not her. Look, Bobby, what are you getting at?"

You lie, he wrote, becoming more telegraphic as he tired. *You see secretly. Jealous! Plain as day. Why lie to me? Why? This* my *house. No lies in my house.*

F.X. examined the note for a moment, then leaned over and pointed to a word his brother had scrawled. "What's this?"

Mr. Pickens printed: MY.

"Oh. *Your* house. Gee, I didn't know this was your house." F.X. looked bemused. "For some reason I always thought it was my dad who paid for it. He's my dad too, remember."

"What!" Mr. Pickens exclaimed, forgetting he couldn't talk. F.X. smiled lazily. "How dare you think, F.X. . . . It was your dad who walked out on my mother. Mother got this house as part of the divorce settlement."

F.X. went to the end table and got another sheet of paper. "Here," he said, handing it to his brother. Going back to the mantel and his drum, he added, "Who said it was part of the settlement?"

"We lived here, didn't we? It must have been."

"Dad never told me this was your house. You got anything in writing?"

"I pay the property tax."

"Thanks. I appreciate it."

"I'm sure Mother has the papers somewhere," Mr. Pickens said, being not sure at all. His mother never did have much of a head for business, and now that she was in a nursing home, she didn't have much of a head for anything. What would she be able to tell him about a divorce that happened thirty-eight years ago when she couldn't even remember having ever been married?

"Bobby, cheer up, son. Long as we're friends, what does it matter?"

Mr. Pickens stared glumly at the bloody porcelain jay.

"Look, now, I really have to know where Toinette is."

Mr. Pickens just sat there, not budging.

"I want to apologize and all."

"I'm not telling," Mr. Pickens said, his jaw immobile.

"What?"

With the stubby pencil Mr. Pickens wrote: *I'm not telling. You can break all the WINDOWS and JAWS in this house, but I'm not telling!!*

About ten minutes later the phone rang. Unfortunately F.X. was in the kitchen and picked it up right away. Mr. Pickens ran into the bathroom for his water glass, then came back and held the glass against the bedroom wall, just opposite the phone in the kitchen. "Yes, baby sweetie," he could hear F.X. saying quietly, "it's all right, the Doughboy's in his room. No, no, you won't be wonely anymore. Daddy's coming to tuck you in. Pontchartrain Courts, right, room seven-sixteen. No, honeypoo, Daddy's not mad no more, he was a bad Daddy, yes, you spank Daddy when he comes. He sorry. Bye, bye, say bye-bye to Daddy."

The center line on the Old Jefferson Davis Highway was painted over an older, faded center line that didn't agree with it; the only way to keep from seeing double and veering into the oncoming lane was to ignore both lines. Mr. Pickens did this, but it seemed an approaching red pickup was having trouble deciding which line to obey. Slowing down as he passed the creosote plant, Mr. Pickens braked hard when the pickup cut right in front of him and skidded into Miss Mina's driveway. Mr. Pickens honked at the driver, who stuck his head out the cab window and vomited. Mr. Pickens drove on.

The night before, while F.X. was supposedly in Ozone again with his parole officer, Mr. Pickens had taken out his file folders and begun a diligent search for a deed or some record that might tell him whose house he was living in. It was a depressing task. Not only had his mother jumbled up all the years—1938 came after 1957—but she had also mixed birth certificates with Luzianne coffee coupons, recipes with canceled checks. All the old phone bills were there, Piggly Wiggly receipts, fliers from J.C. Penney—even the unused ticket to a 1955 demolition derby that Mr. Pickens had been forbidden to attend—but nothing essential: no income tax returns, no legal letters, nothing. How would he ever keep F.X. under control if F.X. thought this was his house too? And what if he never left? What if F.X. decided to make 517 Sweetgum his home, mooching off Mr. Pickens for the rest of his days? Now that Mr. Pickens wasn't dying, there just wasn't any need for an ex-con lolling about the house, smashing windows, dripping blood. No, sir, he could somehow manage to get along without that.

Mr. Pickens was so concerned about the house that all his other worries receded into the background—all except one, Toinette. Now that he knew for sure about her and F.X., there was all the more reason for him to stop those feelings he had for her. The night wore on: his jaw throbbed; he thought of all her bad points; he watched TV; he remembered he was supposed to be looking for something; he tried not to think about the way she touched his jaw; he worried about the house; he started to eat a caramel but had to spit it out because of the pain; he thought some more about her bad points, like the way she slurred over her consonants; he read an old note from his mother in the files (*Bobby, Bobby, why are there no rubber bands in this house? I'm sick and tired of buying them—please train yourself to leave any you come across on the kitchen doorknob*); he searched for the deed. Finally, exhausted, he lay on his bed. Faint traces of her perfume lingered in his room. He closed his eyes; then, to escape the raucous chorus of tree frogs, he buried his head under the pillow.

In the morning, after leaving a note for F.X. telling him he had gone on some errands, Mr. Pickens drove off in his yellow Chevette, heading for the Old Jefferson Davis Highway, where he encountered the swerving pickup.

A few minutes after passing Miss Mina's he was in the next parish, famous for its old plantations, which Mr. Pickens hadn't visited since the outing made by his eighth-grade Louisiana history class. He had made a D on his outing paper and had vaguely resented the plantations ever since. The farms in between these tourist attractions were small and run-down, with hungry, half-wild dogs skulking in the dusty yards. After passing the entrance to the state mental hospital he drove by an emerald field of winter grass, on the edge of which sat an orange and brown Illinois Central pullman car. Its iron wheels were buried in earth, and underneath each window was a flower box brimming with plastic geraniums. MIRACLE CHURCH OF THE MILLENNIUM read the neon sign by the road.

Azalea Manor sat in the middle of a grove of tall, elegant pines. With its two-story columns fronting an old brick-and-plaster facade, it sometimes lured tourists off the highway, curious whether this was a "sight" they should see. After parking near a flagpole Mr. Pickens walked beside a well-tended hedge of camellias, which brought spring to November with a profusion of pinks and reds, until he reached the imposing portico of bull-necked Muses lifting their blank eyes to the heavens. As he informed the nursing home's receptionist that he was there to see his mother, Mr. Pickens wiped a tear from his eyes, which had been invaded by a strong whiff of ammonia.

For ten minutes he sat in the newly modernized lobby waiting for visiting hours to begin. The receptionist had been quite firm about the rule and kept an eye on him as he thumbed through a *Ladies' Home Journal* that seemed to have spent some time underwater recently; it was swollen and pale. Lurking beneath the smell of ammonia was a strange, sweet odor that finally drove Mr. Pickens outside for a breath of fresh air. He wandered about awhile, stopping to inspect a python-thick kudzu that greened a thirty-foot pine trunk. But after plucking a few cicada skins from the bark and crumpling them in his hands, he got bored and returned to the lobby. Next to a large painting of a giraffe done in primary colors was a machine that dispensed combs, rain hats, Vitalis, Brylcreem, and nail clippers. Mr. Pickens went to the receptionist for change for a dollar; he thought he might like a comb. The receptionist told him she wasn't a cashier, so he went back outside and looked at the tree.

Finally, a pink-uniformed girl who couldn't have been much over fifteen escorted him to the elevator. His mother's room was at the end of a long corridor on the second floor. The linoleum here was not as nice as the linoleum in the lobby, and the sweet odor was considerably worse. Down the hall a few feet from them an old man in a wheelchair was crayoning something on the cement-block wall. Without saying a word the attendant jerked the chair around and sailed him into a nearby room. A moment later she rejoined Mr. Pickens, who was trying to decipher the crayon marks on the wall. He couldn't make heads or tails of them—just a bunch of scrawls and something that resembled a fish.

"Come on," the girl said, motioning to him. "Jes' filth, that's all he write, filth." They walked on to the room.

Mrs. Pickens was a tiny woman whose pink scalp shone beneath a smattering of fuzzy baby's hair. When the attendant tapped her on the shoulder and pointed to Mr. Pickens, her mouth made a little O of astonishment. She sat up in bed and buttoned the frilly collar of her nightgown. "A caller," she said, reaching for a reticule on the metal table next to her bed.

"Mother, it's me, Carl Robert," he said a little self-consciously. The attendant was still standing there and watched as Mrs. Pickens opened a mother-of-pearl compact and began repairing her face with Pan-Cake makeup.

The old woman in the room's other bed hoisted herself up on an elbow and asked for a glass of water.

"I done gave you one," the attendant said wearily.

Mr. Pickens frowned at the girl.

"She always axing for water," the girl said, "then she spill it on the floor." With a sigh she poured some water out of a turquoise pitcher and handed it to the old woman. "Here, Miss Jesse," she said sullenly, then left the room.

"Who are you?" Miss Jesse demanded of Mr. Pickens as she dumped the water on the floor. She looked almost twice as old as his mother. One eye was milky—probably from glaucoma—and one side of her mouth drooped down at an impossible angle.

"I'm Mrs. Pickens's son," he said carefully. His jaw still ached, although not quite as badly.

Mrs. Pickens, still applying makeup, tittered. "Oh, Mr. Ames," she said with a wave of her hand, "don't tease poor Miss Jesse."

Mr. Pickens sighed. Mr. Ames was the old man who serviced the vending machines in the Tula Springs area. One day, shortly before she went to Azalea Manor, Mrs. Pickens had called Mr. Ames and asked if she could have a Coca-Cola machine installed in her living room next to the love seat. She said it would be convenient for her guests, especially if the machine was one of the new kind that gave back change.

"Mother," he said firmly, "look at me. I'm Bobby, your son." He stood near the bed, clenching and unclenching his fists.

Mrs. Pickens snapped her compact shut. "I don't want any nonsense out of you, Mr. Ames. You'll upset Miss Jesse." She motioned for him to come closer, then whispered in his ear: "Miss Jesse is dead, but she doesn't know it yet. So be nice to her."

"What did she say?" Miss Jesse demanded.

"Nothing," he said.

"I know what she said." Miss Jesse pointed an accusing finger at her. "She said I was dead. She tells that to everyone."

"Mother, you really oughtn't to say things like that," Mr. Pickens scolded.

Mrs. Pickens wiggled her feet under the electric-orange bedspread, which had a phosphorescent look to it. "Two against one," she sulked. "I suppose you call that fair."

"We're not against you."

"*She* is. She can't stand the fact that I have gentlemen callers. She's just an old-maid schoolteacher—and dead to boot."

Miss Jesse's breathing became labored. She reached for a spray bottle on her table and doused her throat with medicine, then lay back exhausted on her pillow.

"Mama," Mr. Pickens pleaded, pulling up a folding chair next to the bed, "I've got to ask you something important. It's very serious business."

"If it's serious, sir, stop calling me Mama. I am not your mother."

Mr. Pickens looked furtively over his shoulder and saw that Miss Jesse still had her eyes closed. Then he put on a smile and took his mother's hand. "Now, Mrs. Pickens," he said, patting it gently, "I have one little question for you, that's all. See, I can't install the Coke machine in your living room until you show me something that says you are the owner of that house. Do you have a deed, a piece of paper somewhere?" He winked at her.

Mrs. Pickens blushed. "There you go again, Mr. Ames, teasing me like a little rascal. Why, you know I don't live there anymore. Besides, I've given up on Coca-Colas. I've switched to Nehi grape."

"Aha," Mr. Pickens said, trying desperately to sound light-hearted, "so you admit you once had a house in Tula Springs."

"No, Mr. Ames, you know very well I come from Ozone."

He kept a steady pressure on her hand; Ozone was where his mother had grown up.

"And you know very well why I'm not living in Ozone anymore." A distant look came into her eyes.

"Why, Mrs. Pickens? Why aren't you living in that house?" he prompted, hoping to revive some memory in her of having got married.

"Because it's an A&P now. Everyone knows that."

Calling out "Water!" Miss Jesse tried to raise her head.

Mr. Pickens turned to her. "Miss Jesse, are you going to spill it again?"

His mother touched him on the arm. "When she says water, she means hot water. It helps her breathe."

"Where am I supposed to get hot water?"

"Go in the powder room, silly, and use the hot tap."

When he returned with the water, Miss Jesse asked him to crank the bed up so she could sip easier. "I get so dizzy," she said with her head higher now. "Sometimes it seems the whole room is drifting." The loose flesh on the old woman's throat quivered while she drank. "Thank you, Pickens," she said, coming up for air with a gasp. "Yes, I had a Pickens once, taught him Shakespeare."

He tried not to betray his exasperation as she went on: "That was at Ozone High, back before everything got crazy. He wasn't too clever, that Pickens, but oh, my, did he have a smile. I used to make my whole class stand up and smile before we began English. 'Rise and shine!' I'd say, and he'd just smile like the dickens. Sunshine, that's what I called him. He was so sweet, that boy."

Mr. Pickens frowned.

"Oh, oh, the room." She grabbed his hand. "It's coming unmoored. I just hate it when it does this."

Behind him his mother blew her nose with much unnecessary sniffing. "I'm afraid I'm going to have to ask you to leave, Lieutenant," Mrs. Pickens said, dabbing at her eyes with a tissue.

He disengaged his hand from the old woman's and stood up.

"I thought you were a gentleman," Mrs. Pickens said. "But the minute my back is turned, you're . . . Oh, it's too humiliating."

When Mr. Pickens leaned over to kiss her on the forehead, she winced.

"Good-bye," he said, wondering who this lieutenant could be.

"Yes, good-bye. And thank you for the ashes. That's all I've got left, ashes, ashes and ruin and . . ."

"Go, Mr. Pickens," Miss Jesse said over his mother's soliloquy. "Go quick, or she'll never stop."

As Mr. Pickens closed the door behind him he heard his mother say, "Please, Mama, help me," and Miss Jesse reply softly, "Yes, child, I'm here."

CHAPTER

Twelve

Dear Dad,

How are you doing, sir? I am fine as is your other son F.X. who is now out of Angola and living here rent-free at this house with me. F.X. is very sad about his mother who you wouldn't let visit him in jail and who died and was buried without his being able to set eyes on her again, but I understand you must have your reasons for this seeing as what a dissapointment F.X. turned out to be, a disgrace to the entire family. What I don't understand though is how you seem to get me mixed up with him in your mind like I was the one who got sent to Angola. Just because a persons not married is no reason to think he's a common criminal. Lots of famous people were never married like the man who invented penacilon out of stale bread, Warren Beatty, Isaiah, Hamlet, etc. And besides, I'm still counting on getting married and hope it will be soon because I'm so tired of being alone and sometimes I wish I were dead. Sometimes I think everybody just hates me.

I think about you a lot. I think how you tried to get a divorce from me and F.X. only Judge Tilsen wouldn't let you. Was that right, Dad? I just can't square this attitude in my mind with what Jesus teaches us about love and things like that. You always read the Bible at breakfast to me and Mama. Is it fair to make us believe in the Bible and then decide you don't believe in it at all? Cause that's what F.X. told me. He said when his mother told you she didn't think Baptists could get into Heaven, only Catholics, he said that you said to Hell with the whole damn thing and never went to church again. Well, if you ask me that's giving up pretty easy. What if the Pres. of the U.S. said that, just because a Democrat said a bad thing about a Republican? So I really wish you'd stop not writing to me or anything, like I was some sort of public disgrace. And I wish I could find out whose house I'm living in. F.X. claims its your's, but I always thought you gave it to Mama after the divorce. We never talked about finances much, me and Mama, but she always acted like 517 Sweetgum was hers lock, stock and barall. I saw her yesterday and she is fine and sends her love. Please write soon because no matter how mad at you F.X. is and how many bad things he says about you, I always think fondly of you and miss you. (Also, F.X. won't

*get a job. I wish you'd make him get a job so he could pay
for something around here.)*

Your's Truly,
Carl Robert

While waiting for a reply to his letter Mr. Pickens worried
about what he was going to do for a living. There was nothing
in the want ads that interested him, even though F.X. badgered
him about applying for the welding job listed there. "What's
wrong with being a welder?" F.X. wanted to know, but Mr.
Pickens had no intention of going blue collar, no matter how
much it paid. At the mall in Mississippi he told the lady at the
Twin Cinemas box office that he had managerial capacity, and
if she heard that the current manager got sick or was fired or
needed an assistant, would she please keep him in mind. He
loved movies a lot, he explained, and he knew he'd be good at
picking out which ones to show. She told him to move along;
there were people waiting in line behind him.

When he got home from the mall, Mr. Pickens found a pack-
age under the mailbox. It turned out to be the shoe salesman
kit he had sent off for some weeks ago and since forgotten
about. The ad in *Man's Adventure*, which he had been brows-
ing through one day in the barbershop, promised that the
shoes would sell themselves. All you had to do was show your
neighbors the full-color catalog, and before you knew it, you'd
be making hundreds of dollars a week in commissions. Having
already had some experience selling shoes at the mall, Mr.
Pickens had planned on trying this out in his spare time while
working at Sonny Boy. But now that he was fired, it was something of a godsend. He hoped that this, together with his unemployment compensation, would tide him over until he could
find himself a decent job.

The first person he visited with the catalog was his next-door neighbor, Mrs. Wedge. The widow of a chiropractor who was rumored to have been on intimate terms with Huey Long, Mrs. Wedge lived in a pink-brick house with her two cats, Motor and Policeman. She examined the catalog for a moment, then asked Mr. Pickens when he planned to get the cardboard out of his window. She said it hurt her eyes every time she drove by and saw it. He assured her it would be fixed right away. Since the sales kit instructed him to relax and let the customer do most of the talking, he was soon induced to go outside and help her torch a caterpillar tent out of her pecan tree.

"I got the ladder," she said as he felt it wobble under his feet. He was clinging to a pecan branch with one hand while brandishing a homemade torch with the other. The kerosene-soaked rags on the mophead burned with a colorless flame that singed a few gray leaves and left the offending tent intact.

"Can't I just knock it down?" he called down to her bright-yellow hair.

"No." She was a sturdy woman and gave the ladder a warning shake. "They must be burned, Mr. Pickens." She pronounced the word *burned* "boined," the result of having grown up in New Orleans with its Brooklynlike accent.

He climbed closer. Cradled in a sticky, gauzelike pouch, hundreds of pale caterpillars writhed in a hellish tangle. They blackened and curled as he held the mop directly beneath them, until finally the tent broke loose and drifted down. It landed on a sign staked into the manicured rye grass. Yard of the Month, the sign proclaimed. The real Yard of the Month was actually two blocks away at the dentist's new ranch house. Mrs. Wedge had been expelled from the Garden Club because of her forged sign, but she went to their meetings anyway.

At dinner that evening F.X. asked if he had made any sales. Mr. Pickens said he had only called on three people, none of whom needed shoes at the moment. He ate a few more bites of sauerkraut, then noticed through the archway two cardboard boxes sitting by the love seat.

"My weights," F.X. said before Mr. Pickens could ask. "And don't worry, it's my own money."

Mr. Pickens stared at his half-eaten frankfurter. "I got holes in the awnings, cardboard in the window, and what do you throw your money away on?"

"I didn't put the holes in the awnings. As far as the window goes, I'm saving up for it." His eyebrows dipped, then arched high. "Look, Bobby, it's not dumb like you think. I got to look good. How am I going to land a job if I don't look good? I'm an actor."

For a moment Mr. Pickens was too depressed to reply. Then he said, "What sort of job is an actor going to get in Tula Springs? If you're serious about it, then why aren't you in New York or—"

"Mike doesn't like the idea of New York. I got to stay put for a while."

"I don't know, F.X. I just don't know if I can take it much longer."

"You got to have faith in me, son. It's all going to work out. Soon as I get famous, you'll get paid back. I'll give you anything you want."

"It's not just money I'm worried about." With a sigh Mr. Pickens pushed his plate away and folded his arms across his chest. "Are you afraid of her mother, is that it?"

"What are you talking about?"

"Toinette. I know you see her. Please don't try and deny it. It's a waste of breath."

F.X. smiled. "You're back on that one again. Okay, so maybe I have seen her a few times. It's no big deal. I don't really like her that much at all. If I could, I'd call the whole thing off. But you see, she's real hung up on me. She won't let me alone." He leaned closer, then looked over his shoulder as if he were afraid someone might overhear him. "Confidentially, son, the girl just doesn't turn me on. She's too thin, know what I mean?"

Mr. Pickens had no idea what he meant; he really couldn't believe that F.X. didn't find her attractive, not after overhearing that phone call from her at the Pontchartrain Courts. "Listen, F.X., I don't know what you're up to, but whatever it is, you better not hurt that girl."

"You're nuts. What do you mean, up to?"

"I don't know. I just have a funny feeling, that's all."

"They got a name for that funny feeling, Bobby. It's called paranoia. I've seen a lot of guys like you, son. They start out being suspicious of everyone, even their grandmothers, and they end up in padded cells." He raised his eyebrows.

"Well," Mr. Pickens said, fiddling with the saltshaker. He wasn't sure of anything now. Maybe he was crazy after all. Maybe trying not to be in love had done something to his brain. He remembered putting the glass to the bedroom wall: Was that the act of a sane, mature human being?

F.X. stood up and clapped a hand on his brother's shoulder. "I know it's been rough, son, getting fired and all. You've been looking pretty frazzled lately. Why don't you take it easy for a while?"

Although Mr. Pickens was indeed tired and had trouble sleeping, he didn't take his brother's advice. The next day, when F.X. was in the den pretending to study plays he had borrowed from the library (Mr. Pickens suspected it was *People* and *Us* that he really studied; there were stacks of these now in the den), Mr. Pickens sold a pair of Hush Puppies to a pregnant woman in the Hollywood Apartments. Buoyed up by this success, he determined to call on every house on

Sweetgum that day, starting with the Binwangers' on Sweet-gum Extension.

A few minutes later he pulled his Chevette up in front of the ramshackle steamboat Gothic home of R. Vine Binwanger, Tula Springs's former mayor. Mr. Binwanger was something of a controversial figure, since it was under his regime in the late sixties that the town charter had been revoked because of a scandal about garbage collection. Fed up with hauling their own garbage to a dump near Junior's, the residents of Tula Springs had replaced him with a new mayor, who had managed to get back the charter and garbage service just before he was arrested for soliciting minors in New Orleans. Mr. Binwanger, who was now running for mayor again and was expected to win, waved to Mr. Pickens from a widow's walk on the third floor, where he was sitting, reading the paper.

"Pick yourself a satsuma!" Mr. Binwanger hollered down.

Mr. Pickens plucked one off the bush near the Cyclone fence. Although he saw Mr. Binwanger in church every Sunday, he had never spoken to him before and felt a little uncomfortable standing there with the orange fruit in his hand. "Mayor Binwanger?"

"Yes! What can I do for you, son!"

Mr. Pickens hesitated a moment. The sales kit instructions said you were not supposed to tell people you had come to sell them shoes. Rather, you were to be sociable first, then slip it into the conversation as naturally as possible. "How are you doing, Mayor?"

"Speak up!" Mr. Binwanger shouted.

Mr. Pickens shouted back the greeting, then asked if he could come up to talk.

"What do you want!" the former mayor yelled, remaining where he was.

"My name is Bobby Pickens!"

"What do you want!"

"Could I see you for a moment!"

"What for!"

Mr. Pickens's throat was hurting, and his jaw, which had been slowly healing, was now throbbing. "Shoes!"

"What!"

"Shoes!" Mr. Pickens held up his foot and pointed. "Do you need shoes!"

Mr. Binwanger folded his paper in half and leaned back in his chair. "Pick yourself a satsuma!"

Mr. Pickens held up the fruit to show he already had.

"Take another, son!" He waved down, smiling. "Thanks for stopping by!"

Later that morning, after having failed to make a single sale on Sweetgum, Mr. Pickens crossed Flat Avenue to try his luck at Moab's house. The day before, Mrs. Wedge had told him that Moab, her maid, liked to buy shoes, so he figured, why not give it a try? He liked Moab; she always waved to him when she was out sweeping Mrs. Wedge's sidewalk.

Moab lived in a shotgun cabin, two rooms deep, that had an advertisement for Dr. Rigolet's Tonic painted across the windowless side of the house. On the front porch sat a wringer washing machine next to what looked like a large stuffed bear; but as Mr. Pickens got closer he saw that the bear was really a coffee-stained rug thrown over a beanbag chair. Putting a foot on the orange crate that served as a step, he accidentally knocked over a bamboo fishing pole leaning against the porch rail. He froze and, feeling like a prowler, held his breath a moment. He had never been to anyone's house before on this side of the tracks.

He was turning to leave when the rusty screen door, which

had a big gash in it, creaked open. Mrs. Quaid emerged from the dark cabin and stood on the porch, regarding him. Her face looked gray and tired; her slip showed beneath the hem of her faded print dress. "You," she said dully. "What are you doing here?"

Caught off guard, he didn't know what to say. "I was just . . ."

"What's that?" she demanded, taking a step closer.

He looked down at the shoe catalog in his hand, as if he were surprised to find it there. "Nothing."

"Let me see." She reached out and took it from him.

"Nice day," he said while she glanced through it quickly. "Poor old woman's half dead, don't have enough food stamps left for her red beans and rice, and you want to sell her shoes." She tossed the catalog back to him.

"Mrs. Wedge said . . ." He leaned over and picked up the fishing pole. "I didn't expect to see you here, Miss Quaid," he said, hoping to make small talk.

"I bet you didn't."

"You a friend or something?"

"Moab cleans for me, if it's any of your business. She's got a fever, Pickens. I just come by to see how she was."

"Oh."

"And I'm glad I'm here. Last thing she needs is a shoe salesman, fancy shoes. Now, go away, Pickens, git."

"They're not fancy."

"I swear, you're trouble. Seems like every time I turn around, there you are, stirring up another mess. Now, go, shoo." She flicked her hand at him as if he were a bothersome horsefly and went back into the house.

CHAPTER

Thirteen

"Bobby, you been in bed three days now."

Mr. Pickens pushed away the Gatorade F.X. offered. It was noon, and Mr. Pickens was lying in bed with the shades down. He had decided that he was having a nervous breakdown, even though he was not quite sure what a nervous breakdown was. Mrs. Wedge was supposed to have had one a few years earlier from keeping her house too neat, but the only change he noticed in her was that her hair had turned from mousy brown to bright yellow. Whatever the case might be, Mr. Pickens needed something for his misery, and "nervous breakdown" seemed as good a name as any.

"You got to eat something, son," F.X. said while gnawing on a peanut-butter-and-marshmallow sandwich. "You haven't touched a thing in three fucking days."

Mr. Pickens continued to stare at the wall. Actually he had been eating, but never when F.X. was around, because F.X. probably wouldn't understand that you could feel terribly depressed and still want to eat.

"Is there something you'd like me to get you while I'm out?" F.X. asked. "I got to run over to the library, so I could pick up a barbecue or something."

Mr. Pickens pulled the blanket up to his ears and turned his back on his brother, who, with a little grunt, walked quietly out of the room.

As soon as he heard F.X. driving away in the Chevette, Mr. Pickens got up and wandered into the kitchen, where he began to eat potato chips. Still in his pajamas and bathrobe, he walked out the back door for a stroll about the yard. It had continued to be warm for November, but this week it was less humid. The day before, in an attempt to make him feel better, F.X. had raked the lawn, and Mr. Pickens saw now that he had done a surprisingly good job. The ditch looked respectable with the new sods of St. Augustine; all he needed was a wall of cane to shut out the mound of dirt from the Hollywood Apartments' unfinished pool.

Near Mrs. Wedge's sundial a squirrel was nibbling a pecan, while Motor, the cat, crouched a few yards away. Yesterday Motor had killed two squirrels and, as usual, deposited the bodies in Mr. Pickens's yard. (How Mrs. Wedge had trained the cat to do that he'd never understand.) He picked up a pinecone and threw it at the squirrel, which rippled like a nerve impulse straight up the gray pecan trunk.

When he got back inside, he told himself he wasn't going to call Toinette's house to see if she was home. He had a double dose of Nyquil instead, which he used to calm his nerves. Afterward he went and dialed her number. Mrs. Quaid answered, so he hung up without saying anything. It was the third or fourth time he had done that. Once, though, on the day before his nervous breakdown, Toinette had answered. He had asked her if she had found another job yet and if there was anything he could do to help her out. She said yes, quit bugging me—and hung up.

When F.X. got back from the library a few hours later, he came into his brother's bedroom and asked if he'd like to watch TV. There was a good horror show on, and F.X. said he'd fix some popcorn. Mr. Pickens, who had taken another double dose of Nyquil, lay in a dull cloud of misery, unable to sleep, too weary to get up.

F.X. sat down on the edge of the bed. "Look, Bobby," he said softly, staring down at the floor, "I've been trying. I went out to the creosote plant yesterday to see about a job. But hell, man, they wanted me to load these big mothers onto trucks—I mean, you should see those logs. I'm just not cut out for that type of work. I got my career to think about. Mike, you know, he understands. He told me he thinks I could be a real actor. And I'm studying hard, honest. I got Shakespeare out of the library today, like *King Lear* . . . you know, heavy. So listen, you can't let me get to you like this. Okay?"

Mr. Pickens sighed.

F.X. stood up abruptly and opened the shades. "It's so gloomy, no wonder you're down. You got to get out, find yourself a job. That'll cure you, son."

Job. Mr. Pickens thought of Sonny Boy; he had everything back then and he didn't even know it. Toinette was there with him, eight hours a day.

"Hey, you know, I just remembered," F.X. said, clapping his hands. "You've been feeling real tired, right? Do you feel dizzy too?"

Mr. Pickens shrugged.

"Have you vomited at all?"

Puzzled, Mr. Pickens shook his head no.

"What about your hair? Does it seem like you're losing a lot?"

A little alarmed, Mr. Pickens felt his thinning hair. "I don't know. What are you getting at, F.X.?"

"I just read in the Baton Rouge paper the other day. They were talking about toxic wastes, and they had a map of all the dumping grounds. Well, son, one of them is just a mile or so from Junior's. This chemical company from New Orleans has been burying this shit there for years. Didn't you read about the Love Canal? I mean, if the water gets contaminated—that dumping ground looked pretty near to Tula Creek."

"We got springs here, artesian wells. We don't drink out of the river."

"Oh. I guess it's all right, then."

"Of course," Mr. Pickens said, though he was still disturbed by the idea. How ironic it would be if he were really dying of cancer. He brooded a moment: Was he really sure it was his mind that felt bad and not his body? Or could his body have made his brain seem more depressed than it actually was? He sighed and felt more muddled than ever.

F.X. started pacing up and back from the window to the chest of drawers. "Come on, Bobby, you got to get up."

"Leave me alone."

"What are you, boy? Some kind of loser? That's what Dad used to call you, you know. He said you were a loser. He said you didn't have any fight in you. I'm beginning to think he was right."

Stung by this betrayal—how could his father have said that? and yet he always suspected that's what his father thought of him—Mr. Pickens said, "He's right."

"Goddammit, he's not right." F.X. kicked the foot of the bed and then came and grabbed his brother by the arm. "Look here, boy, if anybody has reason to give up, it's me. I'm the one been ruined by the slammer—I'm the one had my mother die on me without so much as a how-do-you-do. So don't give me any more of this nervous-breakdown crap. I've had it up to here." F.X. passed his hand under his chin, then stood there staring hard at his brother. Suddenly, with a wild look in his black eyes, he grabbed Mr. Pickens with both hands and yanked him up.

"F.X.!" Mr. Pickens cried as the buttons popped off his pajamas. But F.X. didn't let go. He hauled him to his feet. "Up, boy, up."

"Don't, F.X., please."

"Take off those fucking pajamas!" F.X. went to the chest of drawers and started flinging clothes out. "This is what you'll wear from now on, normal everyday clothes like normal everyday human beings wear. I said take off those pajamas!"

"I am." Mr. Pickens hurriedly put on a pair of slacks over his pajama bottoms. "See, I'm dressing." He was still afraid F.X. might hit him.

"Feeling sorry for yourself all day," F.X. said grimly, throwing a shirt at him.

The door chimes rang. F.X. told Mr. Pickens, who had put on a white sock and a red sock, to see who it was. Buttoning his shirt up, Mr. Pickens went to the door.

It was Burma from Sonny Boy. She wanted to know if Mr. Pickens wanted to go to Junior's with her. Her fiancé was playing a band concert in Opelousas, and she had to get out of the house because her mother was driving her crazy. Mr. Pickens told her he was sorry—maybe some other time. She lingered on the porch awhile, saying how bad she felt about everybody getting fired. Then she said how she hated Saturdays, when there was nothing to do.

"Good-bye," Mr. Pickens said, shutting the door.

Returning to the bedroom, he was relieved to see that the maniac look in F.X.'s eyes had been replaced by a look of disgust—a definite improvement. "All this time I've been living with you, Bobby, I've been trying hard to see your good side. Look at me when I talk to you. Okay. Now, what did I say?"

"My good side," he muttered, wishing he had the deed to the house in his hands right now.

"You tell me you're going off on dates when you don't

have a girl friend. Fine, I say to myself. It's his life. Then you start telling people I'm your uncle. Okay, I say, let him— it's no big deal. By the way, son, why? Why did you have to do that?"

Mr. Pickens slipped into his loafers. "I . . ."

"Never mind, I don't want to hear. The next thing I know, you're spreading rumors about that Mr. Randy and Toinette, snitching on her like a little punk. You just better be glad you're not locked up in the pen, because I've seen what they do to punks inside. Little punks that snitch, they get a shiv right between the ribs." F.X. picked up a T-shirt lying on the floor and stuffed it back inside the chest of drawers. "Let's see if you can get this room straightened up," he said after opening the window, and then left.

Mr. Pickens sat on the unmade bed, feeling as if his father had just left the room. F.X. did sound like him, but in a heightened sense, almost like a caricature. Mr. Pickens senior wouldn't have used the words *punk* or *pen;* he would have said *weakling* and *Army.* "In the Army, Bobby, they'd take care of weaklings like you." His father wasn't as formidable, physically, as F.X., but he was still taller and heavier than Bobby, and even in his more benign moods he managed to convey a threat of violence. Mr. Pickens sighed; why couldn't everyone leave him alone and let him have his nervous breakdown in peace?

A few minutes later F.X. returned, but Mr. Pickens's bedroom was not ready for inspection. He waited for F.X. to start squawking. "There's a girl here to see you," he said instead, seeming not even to notice the unmade bed.

"I can't see anyone now."

F.X. got his brother's car coat and handed it to him. "You need to get out of the house. You've been cooped up too long."

"Who is it?" he asked, being nudged toward the door.

"I don't know. Just go. It'll be good for you." F.X.'s jaw muscles bulged when he said "good."

When they were in the souped-up Buick riding down Sweet-gum, Mr. Pickens asked Burma why she had come back. Didn't she hear him say he didn't want to go out?

"Don't fuss at me, Mr. Pickens. I can't take it today."

"I said no, plain simple English, *N-O*."

"Well, if you said *N-O*, then what are you doing here with me, anyway?" she asked crossly. The beginnings of her second chin wobbled unpleasantly.

Apparently she was too upset to notice where she was driving, because they weren't headed for Junior's. This was fine with him, since he didn't feel like going anywhere public. They passed the water tower and a discount fireworks stand, and then, in front of a trailer park, she pulled up next to a plywood sign (Strawberry Wine) with a gallon jar of colored water underneath.

"What are you doing?" he asked as her electric window hummed down. He was afraid she was going to steal the jar that was used to advertise the wine. Didn't she realize it was only water with red food coloring?

"My head's spinning," she said. "I can't drive anymore. Mama's got me on a diet for the wedding. She says I can't get married looking like this. You want to drive?"

He changed places with her, but he didn't drive far. A few blocks away, in front of the migrant workers' school, he came to a stop. There was no one around; the school would be empty until March, when the strawberries were ready to be picked.

"What's wrong?" she asked.

"It's not right." He gazed out at the small prefab school. "You got a fiancé, Burma. You should leave me alone."

"But you're my friend."

"I'm not your friend. A man and a woman can't be friends, not until they're old and settled."

"I trust you."

"Why? That's an insult," he said hotly.

"Oh, hush. What sort of fool do you take me for? I know what I look like. The least I can get out of it is having a man friend or two."

Mr. Pickens struggled to say the conventional thing, that she wasn't unattractive, that he did have to guard against his desire for her. But Burma wouldn't listen. "Why is it *really* that you don't want to be my friend?" she persisted.

Your bad grammar, he thought. But it wasn't just that—after all, Toinette's grammar was no bargain.

"Well?" she demanded.

Finally he admitted the truth to himself. It had nothing to do with grammar or tackiness or class, as he used to think. It *was* her looks that bothered him, her body. He could not ignore it, like you were supposed to with friends. Burma's body was always there, a real presence, and to him it was not very appealing.

"I don't know," he said, exasperated with himself as much as with her. He could not tell her the truth; he'd rather be boiled in oil than admit such a thing.

"You're a funny man, Mr. Pickens."

"Bobby—I'm not your boss anymore, remember? 'Mr. Pickens' makes me feel like I got one foot in the glue factory."

"Bobby," Burma said, touching him lightly on the arm. Mr. Pickens wished she wouldn't do that; friends shouldn't touch.

"You asked me earlier why I came back," Burma said a few moments later while they were still sitting in the car. "Well, it was because of your socks. The first time I rung, you came

out trying to act normal, and you had a red sock on one foot
and a white on the other."

Mr. Pickens glanced down at his feet and saw she was right.
"I knew something was wrong."

He coughed. "Nothing's wrong. I just . . ."

She patted the metal curlers under her scarf, then chewed
on a hangnail. "You looked scared or something."

"I can't help it; it's my normal expression, the way my
face is made."

She did not smile. "I don't like F.X. He gives me the creeps.
You ought to get rid of him."

Mr. Pickens felt uncomfortable, as if she were reading his
mind. "Well, he's different, but—"

"You ought to get rid of him."

"Oh, he'll be going, soon as . . . It's just temporary, you
know, the arrangement."

"Get rid of him."

Something in her voice alarmed him. "Burma, why do you
keep on saying that?"

She flung open the car door and got out. He followed her
across the school yard to a canal lined with willows and crab-
grass. On the other side of the canal was a strawberry field
covered with sheets of black plastic, which helped keep down
the weeds. Though it was a cloudless day, the sun looked
distant and pale as a moon. Sitting down, Burma idly stripped
a willow stalk of its slender leaves.

"Bobby," she said, rubbing the brittle leaves between her
hands, "your brother's crazy." She flung the powdered leaves
into the air. "He's nuts."

"Okay, so he's got a temper," he said, sitting down beside
her. "But he's had a hard time."

"What do you mean?"

So she didn't know about Angola. "His mother died and . . ."

"And what?"

"Nothing."

"No, you were going to say something. This is important, Bobby, tell me."

He paused. Toinette had the right to know, didn't she? He wasn't betraying his brother. After all, facts were facts. "He just got out of Angola."

"Oh, Lord," Burma moaned. "I just knew it was something like that. Poor Toinette. What'd he do?"

"Coke."

Her face was a blank.

"Sold cocaine," he explained. "Drugs. Hey, look."

Over the strawberry field drifted a balloon. There was a hot-air balloon club just over the line in Mississippi, and balloons often sailed over Tula Springs. Mr. Pickens waved, but Burma just glanced at it.

"What's the matter?" he asked, feeling alarmed again. She looked at him with large, dilated eyes, and for a moment he was afraid she was going to kiss him.

"What am I going to do?" she asked.

"About what?" *Please don't say you love me,* he tried to convey to her by telepathy. *Please don't.*

"I promised Toinette. I swore I wouldn't tell. She even made me put my hand on the Bible."

Mr. Pickens stood up, his heart beating fast and irregular, his mouth dry. What was she talking about? "Burma?"

"I swore to Jesus I wouldn't."

"Well, don't, then," he said, upset by her distress.

"I got to. I just got to." She grabbed his legs. "Toinette is going to rape F.X."

CHAPTER

Fourteen

On the other side of the canal a stray mutt wandered about, sometimes pausing to sniff and dig in a clump of possum haw. Mr. Pickens was hungrier than he had ever been in the past few days, but he wasn't going to suggest going back to the car until he was sure he had got the story right. Burma had given a patchy, emotional account, skipping over important details that only later questioning on his part had brought out. She had even attempted to stop mid-story because her conscience bothered her. Mr. Pickens was then required to encourage her to go on, which she would do only under one condition: that he promise to be the best man at her wedding.

"But the groom decides that," he had protested. "I don't even know him, hardly."

"Don't worry. Emmet'll decide on you."

"Why, though? Why me?"

"I want you and Emmet to be friends."

It was an absurd request, but he went along with it and heard the rest of the story.

"That dog looks mean," Burma said after she had finished. Mr. Pickens was sitting there with his head in his hands, trying to think. "I hope he don't decide to come over here," she said, sticking a piece of gum in her mouth. "What's wrong with him?"

"Forget about the dog, would you?" he snapped.

"I'm talking about F.X. What's wrong with him? Why would he want to do something so crazy?"

"He was never too bright to begin with, just barely made it through high school. And if it wasn't for his football, he wouldn't have made it at all."

"Yeah, well, I know a lot of people never made it through high school, and they don't think of dumb things like this."

Mr. Pickens nudged a mud-caked oyster shell, which tumbled into the ribbon of water at the bottom of the canal. "I guess he's always had to be the center of attention, can't stand it when anyone else is. When he was out in Hollywood, he said he knew some famous people, his wife did. They used to go to parties where there were movie stars, and you ought to hear him, Burma. Every night he bad-mouths them, tells me this one's a lush, the other one's queer, on and on it goes. He's just green with envy."

Burma patted a loose curler in her hair. "Which ones are queer? Tell me."

"Burma, gossip is the lowest type of communicating; it's for people who aren't very evolved." He took out his handkerchief and gave it to her. "There's a smudge on your cheek there—dirt."

"Oh." From her handbag she got a compact and examined her face in the mirror. "F.X. really knew movie stars?"

"Yeah, that's where he started using coke, so naturally he blames it all on them, going to Angola and all. But I don't think he was ever friends with anyone famous, because when Elizabeth divorced him, he didn't even get to go to the parties anymore. He had to come back to Louisiana to get a job. It must have left a bad taste in his mouth, if you know what I mean."

"I wish I knew someone famous," she said, moistening the tip of his handkerchief with her tongue before dabbing her cheek.

He went on, ignoring her comment. "Then, you know, he's scared to death of turning forty. If you haven't made it by forty, it's all over. I'm so tired of hearing that."

"I'm scared of forty too."

"Not like him. F.X. has a real phobia about it. He's real hung up on his looks too, thinks he's God's gift to woman-kind."

Burma gave him back the handkerchief and snapped shut her compact. "Well, I can't disagree with him there. He is about the most scrumptious man I ever laid eyes on."

Mr. Pickens's face went sour, as if he were jealous. "Come on."

"No, I mean it. Those black eyes of his, they go right through me. I can see why Toinette's a goner. She is totally, insanely wild about him. Remember the first night she saw him, when she was snooping at your window? She claims it was right then she fell in love. That's why she wouldn't let him touch her on their first date. He got so mad he threw her out of your house. Poor girl was real broke up, used to cry on my shoulder practically every night. Then he comes back to her and apologizes, and brother, that's it. He had her wrapped around his little finger in no time. That girl would do anything for him, anything in the world."

"Including rape, huh? She'd actually rape him?"

"No, Bobby, you didn't listen. I told you she wasn't *really* going to rape him—just make-believe rape. And she's still not sure she can do it. She's all mixed up and scared, that's why she told me. She wanted to know if I thought it was crazy. I said, 'Girl, it's not crazy, it's insane. Don't have nothing to do with it.' Then she starts bawling and says if she don't, he'll go away to New York City and she'll never see him again. She says she hasn't got any choice."

They both sat there awhile, silent, as she, frowning with concentration, applied white nail polish to her toes, and he, his lips sometimes moving, carried on a conversation with himself. He still couldn't figure out how a man could be raped, but apparently F.X. had read about this happening once, in Germany. It made all the papers in New York—that's where F.X. got the idea from. And now, according to Toinette, he was boning up on the legal side of rape at the library, working out all the technicalities.

"Listen, Burma," he said aloud. "Give this to me again. You mean Toinette is supposed to be overcome with lust for him?"

Still painting her toes, she sniffed and replied, "Yeah, she's going to testify that he slept with her once or twice but then broke off the relationship because she was too young and he wasn't attracted to her. Only she couldn't stand breaking up with him and started thinking about him day and night until it got to the point where she just *had* to have his body. The funny thing is, it's all sort of true. She's afraid F.X. really isn't in love with her—even though he swears he is—so when she testifies on the stand, it'll sound real because she *is* crazy in love with him. She does love his body and wants it bad. And if she don't rape him—I mean pretend to—she won't have him. He'll leave her."

Mr. Pickens looked up to heaven and sighed. "So that's how he plans to become the big sex symbol. The actor that no woman can resist."

"He's counting on all the papers writing up the trial." She blew hard on her toes.

"Would you stop that? How can you think of toes at a time like this?"

Her eyes went wide with hurt. "Bobby, can't you see? I'm all knotted up inside. I'm just doing my toes to calm my nerves." She stashed the polish back in her handbag.

"Okay, sorry," he muttered. Then, after clearing his throat, he said, "What about Toinette? What if she is convicted?"

"Now think, Bobby. What judge in Louisiana is going to convict a woman of rape? What jury?"

"But still, what about her reputation?"

"F.X. said she'll become famous. And besides, he promised they'd get married after the trial, go away to Hollywood together. And you know Toinette, she's always had her head in the clouds, can't stand Tula Springs. Even before F.X. come down the pike, she used to tell me how different she felt from everyone else, how she had this funny feeling inside her that she was going to be great someday. I guess a lot of that comes from her looks. Do you think she's beautiful?"

He shrugged. The dog on the other bank turned and loped off through the strawberry field.

"Well, I do," Burma said. "I think she's gorgeous. And I hate so bad to see her get mixed up in this. But she's afraid this will be her only chance to get out of Tula Springs. She thinks F.X. might be a sign from God, and if she don't go along with his plan, she'll end up like her mother, all tired and worn out and working in some stupid lunchroom. In a way I can see her point. She *is* too good for us, just too fine a child to go to waste here." Burma leaned back on her pudgy arms and looked up at the soft blue sky. "Hell, Tula Springs is no bargain."

"What's wrong with it?"

"It's dumb, that's all. I'm tired of it myself. If I could go, I'd go." She knocked her sandals together impatiently. "What is there to do here? Nothing 'cept work your butt off, then go home and get soggy. My mama says I drink too much. Emmet says that too. He says once we get married, I'm going to have to cut down."

He watched her profile; there was something clean and pure in its lines that he had never noticed before. Maybe it was because he had never seen her against such a background: beyond her, like in one of those old-time paintings you can see at the museum in New Orleans, there was a hazy blue line of trees. Over them, only a dot now, floated the hot-air balloon. He smelled ozone in the air, that exhilarating whiff you sometimes get after it lightnings a lot. Where had it come from?

"Bobby, do you think you drink too much?"

"I guess so."

"And we're Baptists."

"Modern Baptists can drink. It's only stuffed shirts like Dr. McFlug who don't."

"Well, I guess I'm a modern Baptist, then." She was still looking at the sky. "Want to get drunk?"

"I don't feel like driving anywhere."

She reached in her handbag, which was big as an overnight bag, and pulled out a quart bottle of Old Crow. But the liquid inside was dark, not at all like bourbon. "I've taken up Toinette's drink," she said, unscrewing the cap. "Bourbon and Tab cola. Do you mind drinking from the same bottle? Here, you first."

He took a swig. His head buzzed immediately; the saccharin in the Tab seemed wonderful.

"Hey, leave some for me," she cried happily.

Ten minutes later, sprawled on his back, he felt as if he were cradled in the basket of the balloon, floating high above the clean-scented pines. F.X. was crazy, Toinette was crazy, Burma was crazy—but somehow it didn't matter so much now.

He no longer worried that F.X. would actually go through with his scheme and ruin everyone's life. After all, who would believe such a story?

"That's where you come in," Burma said after he had told her his thoughts. She was undoing her curlers, putting them one by one into her scarf and brushing her brown hair vigorously.

"Me?"

"Bobby Pickens, prime witness for the prosecution." She took another healthy swig from the half-empty bottle. "Upstanding churchgoer, well-respected citizen, never been in no scrapes with the law—yes, you." She talked through the bobby pins in her mouth. "You'll be sitting at home one night—soon as you get over your nervous breakdown—and . . ."

Even though he was drunk, he blushed—and tried to figure out how she knew: F.X. told Toinette, who told Burma? It seemed complicated to his fuzzy brain.

". . . Toinette comes pounding on the door saying she's got to see F.X. You hear them arguing, F.X. saying how he can't see her anymore because she's too young and he doesn't love her, then you hear her getting hysterical. The next thing you know some big lug is going to tie you to a chair, and then he's going to drag F.X. into the bedroom and tie him to the bed."

"Hold on, what big lug?"

"Toinette's not sure. She thinks it might be some friend of F.X.'s. Wouldn't be hard to find someone, not if what you tell me is true about Angola and all. Pay him a few bucks, then let him disappear. He won't be in the trial or anything." All the curlers were out, gleaming dully in the pale sun. "Anyway, the next thing you hear is all these sighs and groans coming from the bedroom. I guess you'll be tied up in the kitchen so you can hear good. Then at the trial F.X. is counting on you just telling the truth about what happened to you. See, you won't be committing perjury or anything. You'll just be you, because you won't know anything about the plan. I have to admit, Bobby, no matter how dumb you say F.X. is, that part sounded pretty good to me. I mean, I can just see you there"—she giggled—"telling the truth."

He propped himself on one elbow and regarded her. "You think for one second I'd have anything to do with this plan?"

"Not if you know, which is why I'm telling you."

Satisfied, he lay on his back again. A large bird, probably a hawk, soared up over the tree line without moving its wings. He watched it contentedly for a moment.

"I know you're a man of high morals," she said, stuffing her scarf and curlers in her handbag. "You wouldn't let anything stand in your way of stopping this thing, would you?"

"Course not."

"That's what I thought. The most important thing is helping Toinette, right?"

"Right."

"You know, of course, you can't let F.X. know you know."

"Say that again."

"You can't just tell F.X. not to do it." She fought against her large unnatural curls with her brush. "See, he told Toinette not to tell anybody. He said if she did, he'd ruin her good. So she wasn't supposed to tell me, and so you're not supposed to know either."

He reached for the bottle, thinking another drink might help him straighten this tangle out. "What'll I do, then? How can I stop him if I can't tell him I know?"

She cleared her throat. "That isn't the hard part. I'm fixing to tell you the hard part."

"What?"

"Now, remember, Bobby, you told me you were moral and nothing would stop you from helping her."

His sense of chivalry, swollen by now with bourbon and Tab, blustered forward: "I wish you'd stop saying that. Of course I'm going to help her. I'd do anything for that girl, anything in the world, and—"

"Okay, okay, hon." She laid her hand over his mouth. "Just listen a second. You know that watch?"

"What watch?"

"The watch you stole from Toinette."

"I never stole any watch from . . ." he cried while inside him something shriveled up very rapidly.

"Hush. Let me just give you the facts. Toinette's always suspected you, and she told F.X. Anyway, F.X. found it in your bottom drawer in the dresser. He plans on using it against you if you refuse to be a witness or anything. Understand?"

Quietly, trying to still his heart, he said, "But I didn't steal it. I was always planning to give it back to her—it was just a game, a joke. I just wanted to get her attention, but she ran to Mr. Randy before I could explain, and then . . ."

"It's all right, Bobby," she said, smoothing his hair. "I understand. The trouble is, F.X. is going to make Toinette press charges if you don't go along. Now, that's not going to bother you any, is it? I mean, all you'll have to do is tell the police the truth, tell them you didn't really steal it."

"I tried to put it back in her purse, but then we were both fired, and I couldn't see her anymore because she wouldn't speak to me, and . . ."

"Calm down." She pulled a Kleenex out of her handbag and mopped his forehead. "It's all right."

Mr. Pickens looked up. The hawk was gone; the sky was blue and empty now, except for the sun, which had grown larger, flushed with a tinge of orange. "I don't know," he whispered.

"What?"

The ground tilted beneath him; he reached out to regain his balance and latched onto her arm. He was very drunk.

Part
TWO

"Time and chance happeneth to them all."
—Ecclesiastes 9:11

Fifteen

If there was one thing Donna Lee Keely tried to impress upon her family, it was the importance of reality. Her parents had a way of forgetting what the world was really like, and Donna Lee, because she loved them, felt it her duty to remind them. When she was an English major at Sophie New-combe, her weekend visits were often peppered with these gentle reminders: "Dad, right this minute children are starving in the Sudan, and you have to have another bowl of gumbo?" Or to her mother, who was upset over a scratch Donna Lee had made in the new teak coffee table: "Hundreds of people have just been killed in that earthquake in Turkey, Mother, and you're worked up over a little scratch."

After college Donna Lee applied to the Peace Corps, but turned down an offer to go to Nigeria because of her stomach. It was extremely sensitive in those days and gave her a chronic case of diarrhea and gas pains. Instead she went to Tulane Law School, where she fell in love with an urban planner twenty years her senior. He was a diffident man who led her on for two years without ever declaring his love for her, and left her, when she graduated, deeply wounded and exhausted. Returning to Tula Springs, she found a small apartment about a mile from her parents' house and got herself a job in Mr. Herbert's law office. The job, of course, was only temporary, something she would do while she recovered from the urban planner. In the back of her mind was a vague plan to move someday to New Orleans or maybe Atlanta, where she would find a more high-powered job.

Mr. Herbert was a kind, precise man who encouraged Donna Lee to wear a dress or skirt in the office. Other than that he let her go pretty much her own way. She was bright and well organized. Her only fault was a tendency to get over-involved with clients, especially divorce clients, who were treated to long, emotional lunches at the mall in Mississippi. She would make up for these by working late at the office, then straggle in an hour late the next morning. Mr. Herbert liked to close up at five on the dot and felt nervous about Donna Lee's working there alone, afraid that her electric teapot might somehow start a fire.

One Friday afternoon, just as Mr. Herbert was preparing to leave for the weekend, Mrs. Pickens's son dropped in. Mr. Herbert did not think much of either Mrs. Pickens or her son. As far as he was concerned, Mrs. Pickens should have been institutionalized from Day One. And as for Bobby, it was time he shaped up or shipped out. The boy had no spirit, no get-up-and-go. He always looked rumpled and dazed, as if he had just arisen from a long midday nap. If it weren't for the fact that Mr. Herbert's wife was related to Mrs. Pickens—a second cousin or something—Mr. Herbert would have been far less tolerant of these visits with her son, which were usually un-billed chats for a little free advice. This evening, anxious to get home for a bite before his son's high school volleyball tournament, he was a little more impatient than usual. After exchanging a brief greeting with Mr. Pickens and a few obser-vations on the weather, he guided him into Donna Lee's office. Donna Lee had not shown up until ten thirty that morning, so Mr. Herbert did not feel too bad about pawning Mr. Pickens off on her.

"Donna Lee, better not bother coming in on Saturday," Mr. Herbert said before he left. "The workmen will be here to fix the leak in the roof." He smiled at Mr. Pickens as he backed out of the office. "Good evening, sir."

Donna Lee had stood up when the two men entered her office. Because she was thin and large-boned, she gave the impression of being taller than she actually was. Her face, though, was round, almost moonish, with soft, very feminine features. When she was alone with Mr. Pickens, she settled back into her desk chair. Mr. Pickens just stood there.

"Why don't you sit down?" Donna Lee said, gesturing toward the pew in her office. It was a small Lady chapel pew that she had found in an antique shop on Toulouse Street in New Orleans. There were no pictures on the wood-veneer walls of the office, or curtains on the one window, which looked down on a shoe repair shop's tin roof.

"Well, actually . . ." he began, testing out the pew. It sloped a little and was very smooth; clients tended to drift about on the shiny mahogany during their interviews, trying to find a comfortable position. "I just came to say hello to Mr. Herbert. Nothing important, really."

Donna Lee regarded him a moment with her dark-blue eyes. Overnourished people did not appeal to her; neither did slack, vague expressions. And that leisure suit he had on was appalling: blue and green checks, initials on the lapel . . . "Is Mr. Herbert a friend of yours?" she asked through a tight smile.

"Huh?" he said, gazing about the room. Outside a sudden breeze caused some chinaberries to fall with a rattle onto the tin roof. "Oh, he's my cousin."

"I see. Well, is there anything I can help you with?"

He cleared his throat and adjusted a strand of hair that strayed down his forehead. "I was hoping we could talk sort of unofficially."

"I'm sorry, Mr. Pickens, but my meter went on the minute you walked in this office. You're already paying for an hour's worth of me, so you might as well use it."

"But . . ."

"If Mr. Herbert wishes to make some adjustment, that's between you and him. Now, tell me, what is your problem?" Donna Lee was talking in what was for her an unnaturally gruff voice. This was because only a few minutes ago, just before Mr. Pickens came in, she had been experimenting with a new Dictaphone and was shocked by the way she sounded—so breathy, almost like Marilyn Monroe.

Folding his arms across his chest, Mr. Pickens slouched forward a little. "I really hadn't counted on this," he muttered to the floor. "You see, uh, currently I seem to be unemployed. I was formerly, at one time, the manager of a large department store, but I decided I needed a more challenging position, if you know what I mean."

She did; he was probably fired.

"Anyway, it's my house I'm worried about. See, I've lived there all my entire life, then all of a sudden from out of the blue F.X. up and says . . ." Mr. Pickens's voice choked up, forcing him to pause for a moment. Recovering, he continued, keeping his eyes fixed on the new indoor-outdoor carpeting, which Donna Lee hated; it was bright as Astroturf. "I'm sure it belongs to my mother, the house, only I can't find the right papers or anything. I went over to City Hall, but this secretary there was real rude. She told me she didn't know what I was talking about and—"

"If it's the title deed you're after, go to Ozone, the parish courthouse. Check with the Department of Records. And also, if your house is mortgaged, the bank should have those records."

"It's not that simple, really. See, my mother got divorced

a long time ago, and that's when the house must've been transferred over to her. But I can't find the divorce papers."

"Was Mr. Herbert her lawyer then?"

"No, ma'am. He was about ten years old back then. I was barely born."

Donna Lee asked why he couldn't get this information from his mother or father. Mr. Pickens explained that his mother's mind wandered and that his father was living incommunicado in Tucson.

"Incommunicado?" she asked, trying to suppress a yawn.

"Won't answer any of my letters, and his phone's unlisted." He looked up, and for a moment it seemed he was trying to read upside-down a deposition lying on her desk.

"Mr. Pickens."

"What? Oh. Well, I don't know what's wrong with him. A couple years ago he tried to divorce us, me and F.X. But Judge Tilsen wouldn't let him."

"Who's F.X.?"

"My half brother. My father married an Italian lady, and they had F.X. down in Ozone."

"And F.X. is the one saying your house is his?" Donna Lee said wearily. Had she heard right, was the father divorcing the sons? No, she must be tired, losing track.

"Yes, ma'am, F.X. thinks he owns the world, thinks he can do whatever he likes and . . ."

Donna Lee reached in her purse and pulled out a tissue, which she handed across the desk to Mr. Pickens. Avoiding her eyes, he took it, dabbed at his pale eyes, and blew.

"Listen, Mr. Pickens. I suggest you go to the courthouse in Ozone. If that doesn't work, come back and see me, okay?"

He nodded but remained in the pew.

"And listen, hon, don't worry about a bill," she said, standing up and extending her hand. "Have a nice weekend."

Mr. Pickens remained seated, not seeing the hand.

"Mr. Pickens?" she said a little testily.

"Oh," he said, and then with a muddled look on his face sidled past her out the door.

For a few minutes Donna Lee worked on a will for Mrs. Jenks's handyman, Mr. Ray, whom she had visited earlier in the day. The will was a royal pain in the ass. Mr. Ray wanted to give all the money he had—$123.28—to the U.S. Army and all his vintage 1940 sharkskin suits to J.C. Penney. She worked in the office till seven, drinking several cups of shave grass tea, then packed up the briefs she would work on over the weekend and locked the office.

CHAPTER

Sixteen

That evening after work Donna Lee had dinner at her parents' house, which was roomy and comfortable, but plain-looking, almost severe, when seen from the street. Mrs. Keely had forgotten she had invited her daughter to dinner; this meant that Mr. Keely had to do without seconds on his favorite dish, stuffed peppers. During the meal Donna Lee's father, an officer at the Tula Springs Savings and Loan Association, gazed vacantly out the bay window whenever the conversation lagged.

"How was work?" Mrs. Keely asked for the third time as she passed her daughter the coleslaw. Donna Lee's mother was a little distracted because she was trying to keep the

names of the gods and goddesses straight in her mind. She
had a test on Monday at St. Jude State College, where she
was auditing classes in mythology and abnormal psychology.

"Mother."

"Oh, yes," Mrs. Keely said vaguely. In her early sixties,
she was a striking woman, buxom, with a head of long snow-
white hair gathered in a chignon. Donna Lee envied her
mother's knack of appearing gracious and composed no matter how she was feeling.

"Dad, have you ever heard of the Calydonian boar?" Mrs.
Keely said to her husband, who was humming—unconsciously,
as usual—"Three Blind Mice." Hypnotherapy, a birthday
gift from Donna Lee, had failed to cure him of this awful
habit. Mr. Keely, though, assumed he *was* cured and was always surprised when someone asked him to stop humming.

"Yes?"

"I asked if you had heard of the Calydonian boar." Mrs.
Keely dabbed at her cheek with a napkin; she dabbed fre-
quently during meals, even though there was nothing to dab at
but a spotless creamy-white cheek. "This boar was a dread-
ful beast, very large and unpleasant. Many, many good people were upset by it. So one day the men of the town gathered
together and said—"

"What town?" Mr. Keely asked. "There's some pretty big
boars right outside Ozone."

"Don't interrupt. Anyway, there was a young lady, re-
nowned as a top athlete—"

"Mother," Donna Lee said.

"She threw the javelin as far as—"

"Mother, you put sugar in the coleslaw."

"I forgot you were coming to dinner."

"But it's not just me. Think of Dad. He's overweight, he's
got high blood pressure, and you feed him sugar."

"Oh, I'm so tired of sugar. That's all we ever talk about, sugar and chemicals."

"Look what time it is," Mr. Keely said, glancing up at the cuckoo clock over the sideboard. When she was eight years old, Donna Lee had stolen the cuckoo, then lost it, so that now only a silent stick of wood, its perch, heralded the hour. "They'll be here any minute."

"Who's they?" Donna Lee asked.

"Dad's Bible study class," Mrs. Keely said. "He's always volunteering our house."

"We rotate, dear," Mr. Keely said patiently. He scratched absently at a freckle on his broad face.

"Well, I don't understand why you can't rotate yourselves over to the church hall. That's what it's there for."

"Did you get any refreshments like I told you?"

"Last time they crumbed up my living room so bad," Mrs. Keely said to Donna Lee, pretending not to have heard him, "Moab and I never did get it back to normal. I kept on discovering little crumbs behind the cushions. Hey, Dad, where are you going?"

Mr. Keely, halfway out of his chair, sank back into it. "Dr. Henry's."

"Must you feed them?"

"Oh, Mother, I'll go." Donna Lee got up.

Her father handed her a few bills from his wallet. "Be sure and get enough. They like that blue-cheese dip. And get the king-size Fritos. Not the little ones. And plenty of root beer and 7-Up. Here, take another five, just in case."

"Finish this slaw for me," Mrs. Keely said to her husband, and then, as Donna Lee was going out of the dining room, she called out, "Don't be extravagant."

The door to the cuckoo clock opened, and the stick came out.

"Oh, look, Leon," Mrs. Keely said, peering out the bay window. "She's taking your bike, and it doesn't have a light."

Mr. Keely began humming again.

Donna Lee sat in the kitchen with her mother, who had her Edith Hamilton open on the oak table, while the men talked about the Bible in the next room. Donna Lee kept threatening to go in there and tell them what *she* thought of that Bible. "It really gets me, Mother. The ones who are the worst racists are always quoting the Bible."

Mrs. Keely highlighted a passage in her book with a yellow Marks-a-Lot.

"How Dad can associate with those people, I don't know."

Mrs. Keely looked up, her bright-blue eyes full of puzzlement. "I wonder, did Moab say she was going to buy some Top Job?" Moab came twice a week to help Mrs. Keely clean.

Suddenly the men in the living room burst into laughter.

"Probably just told a nigger joke," Donna Lee commented.

"Dear, please," her mother said with a pained expression.

"I saw Mrs. Jenks today. You know, that woman who writes for the paper."

"Oh, yes. I'm always running into her at the beauty parlor."

"Do you realize her poor handyman is starving to death? Right here in Tula Springs we've got someone starving to death. And she won't even sign him up for food stamps."

"Well, dear, you *know* what people buy with food stamps— the most expensive brands. Just the other day, at the A&P, the woman right in front of me had two bottles of Progresso olive oil. Progresso. Why, I wouldn't dream of anything but that unlabeled kind. It's such a blessing, all that no-brand food they have. They're in the white cans, Donna Lee."

"Mother, can you be real for a minute? This man must

weigh only seventy, eighty pounds. It's too awful. I told Mrs. Jenks it was like Auschwitz."

"I hope you didn't." The freezer on the other side of the spotless kitchen began to clank; Mrs. Keely gave it a worried look. "That's not a very nice thing to say to someone. Poor Mrs. Jenks has to manage all by herself."

"Ha, that's a joke. She's got maids coming out of her ears, black women who should be going to college, not ironing a silly old woman's underwear."

The kitchen door swung open. Mr. Keely came in and started going through the cupboards over the sink he was allowed to use when he needed to scrub his hands after yard work. The other sink, newly done over in stainless steel, was off limits.

"What are you looking for?" Mrs. Keely asked.

"I thought we had some potato chips," he said vaguely, his back to them. "Cookies, anything."

"Really, Leon, after all the trouble Donna Lee went to," Mrs. Keely said, shaking her head. Donna Lee had decided the Bible class didn't need junk food, and brought back apples, carrots, and cauliflower instead.

"Dad, can I come listen in?" Donna Lee asked.

"You let your father be," Mrs. Keely said.

"Dad?"

With a dejected air Mr. Keely gave up the search. "What, honey? Well, sure."

"But it's a *men's* Bible class," Mrs. Keely objected. "It's time Donna Lee was on her way home. I can't get any studying done with her around."

"Ann, you know Donna Lee is welcome here anytime she wants, for as long as she wants. It's her house." He winked at his daughter. "You know your mother doesn't mean it."

"Foolishness," Mrs. Keely said, returning to her book.

•   •   •

"Dr. McFlug, I believe you know my daughter, Donna Lee."
Donna Lee held out her hand to the old doctor, whose stiff,
lusterless dyed brown hair, worn stylishly long, fooled people
into thinking it was a wig. Tall and spindly, he didn't seem to
realize what she intended until she grabbed his hand and gave
it a firm, manly squeeze. The other men remained standing
until Donna Lee pulled up the bench from the Mason & Ham-
lin baby grand and sat down. Next to her father on the over-
size couch was Mr. Binwanger, Tula Springs's ex-mayor, and
beside him, Mr. Dambar, the owner of the creosote plant out
on the Old Jefferson Davis Highway. Squeezed into her
mother's favorite wing chair was a fat, florid-faced man she
had never met before who was introduced to her as Mr. Randy.
In the Windsor chair sat his brother-in-law, Mr. Gaglioni, who
didn't look very Baptist to Donna Lee.

"This is his first time," Mr. Randy said to her, jerking a
thumb at his brother-in-law, who smiled weakly back at her.
"He's my new assistant manager over at Sonny Boy. Want
to help him mix and mingle. Say hello, Sal."

"Hello," the young man mouthed silently. He sat stiff as
a board, his back not touching the chair.

"Gentlemen," Mr. Keely said after clearing his throat,
"since we're all agreed you are an exceptionally bright, intelligent group of citizens, I'm sure you'll welcome the addi-
tion tonight of a pretty face." He gestured toward his
daughter, who gave him a sour look. She had tried, tried
very hard, but despite her best efforts, it seemed her father
would never recover from the Dale Carnegie course he had
taken thirty years ago.

"Dr. McFlug," Mr. Keely said, unfazed by his daughter's
look, "I believe we were all enjoying your reading. Where did
we leave off?"

The old doctor glared at his Bible and brought it up to

within an inch of his face. " 'Moreover there were at my table an hundred and fifty of the Jews and rulers, beside those that came unto us from among the heathen that are about us. Now that which was prepared for me daily was one ox and six choice sheep; also fowls were prepared for me, and once in ten days store of all sorts of wine: yet for all this required not I the bread of the governor, because the bondage was heavy upon this people.' "

Donna Lee leaned forward on the bench, her eyes closed, listening hard. When Dr. McFlug paused to mop his brow with his handkerchief—he put a lot into his reading, each word sounding heavy as a brick—she raised her hand. "Did you say that this man ate a whole ox every day?" she asked.

"And some sheep and chickens," Dr. McFlug said.

"Well, no wonder he doesn't require the bread of the governor, not after all that. My God, who is this man?"

"Nehemiah," Dr. McFlug said, reaching for the apple juice Donna Lee had provided.

"Now, Donna Lee, the ox wasn't just for him," her father said with an anxious smile. "There were two hundred other people at his table."

"An hundred and fifty," Dr. McFlug corrected, then held up the book again. " 'Think upon me, my God, for good, according to all that I have done for this people.' "

"Some good," Donna Lee put in. "He takes the choice sheep and fowl and leaves everyone else the bread."

"I think you're missing the point," Dr. McFlug said calmly. "Nehemiah was engaged in building a wall at that time. He was a good governor."

"Would you think it good," Donna Lee persisted, "if Mr. Binwanger had taken all the meat from your table when he was mayor and left you nothing but bread?"

" 'Bread' probably means something else," Mr. Dambar

said. He was a good-looking man who sometimes took Mr. Keely shrimping in Lake Pontchartrain. "At least in this passage 'bread' doesn't mean actual bread."

"Neither do I," Donna Lee said, smiling at Mr. Binwanger, who, having had his mind elsewhere for the past half hour, smiled back at her. Mr. Binwanger would probably be re-elected mayor, mainly because of his law-and-order campaign. He promised to give Tula Springs a police force, although where he'd find the money for it, God only knew. Tula Springs couldn't even afford to get the sewer main fixed over on South Street where the live oak roots had busted through a culvert.

"Pardon me, Mr. Dambar," Dr. McFlug said coolly, professionally, "but I believe if Nehemiah said bread, he meant bread. We just can't go substituting words in Scripture, now, can we?"

"Correct," Donna Lee said, scooting the piano bench a little closer. "Either you believe what's written there, just like it says, or you don't. Either it's the word of God, or it isn't."

Dr. McFlug nodded solemnly while Mr. Keely opened his mouth to say something, then shut it. A vague, low hum stirred the air.

Mr. Randy's pudgy fingers strayed to the plate of raw cauliflower next to his chair, violating one of Mrs. Keely's edicts: If you touch it, you must eat it. Fiddling with the cauliflower, he said, "This is Pickens's fault. He was supposed to do Nehemiah this week, read up on it for us. And it's twice he's skipped out having us over to his house. Sal, *here*," he concluded, handing his brother-in-law a handful of white flowerets.

"Mr. Gaglioni," Donna Lee said, "what do you think about the bread?"

His back still away from the chair, his mouth full of cauliflower, the young man looked with a pained expression at his brother-in-law. Mr. Randy scowled at him. "Don't ask Sal here nothing, Miss Keely," Mr. Randy said, rubbing a huge, bushy eyebrow with his knuckle. "He still hasn't caught on to the language too good."

"Oh, sorry," Donna Lee said, getting up. "Would everyone like more apple juice?"

"How about Dr Pepper?" Mr. Randy asked.

'I'm afraid all we have is apple juice."

"All right, I'll take some of that."

When Donna Lee returned from the kitchen, where she had a quick spat with her mother, who had been eavesdropping on the Bible class, Mr. Binwanger was explaining to Mr. Dambar the best way to skin a catfish: "You got the nail hammered in the tree, head high. Okay, next you hook the cat up there by its gill, right? Then slice just around the gills with your knife, grab off a piece of skin with your pliers, then yank down for all you're worth. Oh, thank you, hon," he said, taking a glass of juice from Donna Lee. "Best if you skin it while the bugger's still kicking."

"Gentlemen," Mr. Keely said, "I believe Dr. McFlug was saying something very intriguing."

Dr. McFlug took a gulp of the apple juice that Donna Lee had just set down in front of him, then another large gulp. "An ox divided into a hundred and fifty portions would probably be equal to about a pound of meat per man. I trust Miss Keely would not find this offensive, one pound per day, probably not much more than thirteen hundred calories."

"Dr. McFlug," Donna Lee replied as he finished the apple juice in a few more gulps, "since when do oxen weigh only a hundred and fifty pounds?"

"We aren't counting the head and legs and insides. Only the choice meat."

"Let's say that's another hundred and fifty, the ox still weighs only three hundred pounds. I defy you to show me a three-hundred-pound ox. Plus there's all that sheep and fowl."

"I think you're missing the point," Mr. Keely said.

"Dad, an ox weighs at least a thousand pounds, maybe even a ton."

Mr. Keely leaned forward and took the Bible from Dr. McFlug's lap. "Here," he said, pointing a thick finger at the text. "It says there were a hundred fifty Jews '*beside* those that came unto us from among the heathen.' So you see, Donna Lee, that could mean there were a thousand all together."

"More, please," Mr. Gaglioni said to Donna Lee, holding out his empty glass.

"Sal," Mr. Randy reprimanded.

"Say, while you're up, maybe you could get me some more too," Dr. McFlug said. "I'm parched."

Donna Lee went back to the kitchen and while her mother wasn't looking poured a healthy dose of vodka into the two glasses, which she then filled with apple juice. When she had gone back to the kitchen earlier, she had decided to give Sal a little booze because she couldn't stand to see someone sitting so straight that his back wouldn't touch the chair. Then she had decided Dr. McFlug could use something to loosen him up too. The rest of the men, like good Baptists, got straight apple juice.

In the living room catfish had strayed into the conversation again. When Mr. Keely steered them back to Nehemiah, Mr. Binwanger sagged back against the sofa cushions with a glazed look in his eyes.

"Boy, where's your manners?" Mr. Randy said as Mr. Gaglioni drained his glass in a few gulps.

Dr. McFlug looked sharply at Mr. Randy. After polishing

off his third glass of apple juice Dr. McFlug began to sound like the Bible even when he wasn't reading. If God willed, he proclaimed to Donna Lee, an ox could weigh three hundred pounds.

"*Prego, signora.*" Mr. Gaglioni held out his glass to her. She stood up and took his and Dr. McFlug's into the kitchen for refills.

When Donna Lee returned, the ox had shrunk from three hundred to fifty pounds, then one pound—if God willed. No one seemed too concerned with the one-pound ox except Mr. Keely, who had an odd look on his face as he strained to follow Dr. McFlug's inspired commentary.

When she saw that Mr. Gaglioni was slouching comfortably in his chair, Donna Lee excused herself and went into the kitchen to say good night to her mother.

"Are they using the çoasters I put out?" Mrs. Keely asked without looking up from her book.

"Bye, Mother," Donna Lee said from the door.

"They better not leave any rings on my furniture," she said as her daughter closed the door behind her.

CHAPTER

Seventeen

Saturday afternoon Donna Lee drove fifty miles south to Ozone for a Sierra Club meeting. On the agenda that day was a discussion of the toxic chemical wastes at Tula Creek. For years the dumping had gone on illegally, but now the town of Tula Creek was going to do something about it. At a recent session the town council had voted to collect a special tax from the chemical companies for dumping on city property and thus make the whole thing legal. This explained where the money for a police force would come from. The Sierra Club was livid with Tula Springs, and as a lifetime member, Donna Lee was officially livid too. But she was too depressed to work up any real lividness. The urban planner was troubling her again. The wound seemed fresh even though just yesterday she had felt cured, whole again. She wondered if she would ever recover. Listless, unstrung, she signed the petitions and donated fifty dollars to the cause, but she did not volunteer for the task force that would smash Mr. Binwanger and his cronies on the Tula Springs town council.

The meeting over, Donna Lee drove along the lakeshore, not ready to return to Tula Springs yet. The lake reminded her of the urban planner; it was the reason she didn't settle in Ozone, which was so much nicer than Tula Springs. Tula Springs was Baptist, puritanical, its houses either dowdy or plain. Ozone, though, had one mansion after another along its lakefront, lavish houses that looked like wedding cakes piled high with sweet, useless fancy. Many of them were empty, of course, or only half used, an upper floor sealed off because of the heating bills. In one of these houses, built like the Jefferson Davis house in Biloxi, lived, or used to live, a great-aunt of Donna Lee's. As Donna Lee passed it now she remembered the day— she was nine then—the old woman had taken her aside and whispered in her ear: "Yesterday I saw hummingbirds sliding down the wax myrtle out in the front yard, just having themselves a ball. But don't you dare tell anyone, Donna Lee. They'll think I'm nuts."

A half mile later she came to the old riverboat that used to ferry people across the great gray plain of the lake to New Orleans. It was a restaurant now. She and the urban planner had eaten there often. The food wasn't that good, but when you looked out the window, there was no land in sight, and that's why they ate there. She was always too happy to really eat, though. It was a strange happiness, bobbing gently over wave after wave of nostalgia. Not that the urban planner reminded her of anyone. He didn't; no one could be like him, so perfect, so invulnerable. Yet still he managed to sound depths in her, of a past she had forgotten, of old loves, longings that were never satisfied.

Just ahead of her was the Ozone Lux, the screen like a blank billboard with tears in a few spots that showed the ribbing underneath. It was here that he had first made love to her, furtively, with a station wagon full of kids next to them. The movie was a horror film, ants or bees or something swarming over terrible actors. Donna Lee slowed down. The tall brown grasses that now covered the parking lot were stroked by a gentle breeze from the lake. Rolling down the window, she breathed in this air and imagined she could pick out, among the tang of salt and evergreen mixed with the duller scent of leaf mold, the pungent aroma of his body that night when the kids in the station wagon were squealing and whining so fearfully close to them.

She did not go up the ramp to the expressway north but turned around and retraced the almost deserted lakefront drive. Once or twice the Volvo rumbled onto the grass shoulder of the asphalt, but it didn't really matter, since she was going so slow. She passed the riverboat restaurant again; a man in an unseasonable white suit walked down the gangplank. Her great-aunt's house: there was no wax myrtle in the yard now, just unkempt grass and what looked like an overturned sink.

A few miles outside Ozone the St. Jude campus began. Donna Lee remembered that near the Black Angus Coliseum was an unusually large patch of yaupon. Yaupon leaves made a unique tea, which she gave to her family and friends at Christmas, warning them, though, by means of a special label on the canister, that too many cups of this aromatic, really tasty all-natural tea made you vomit—so take it easy, two cups at a sitting, the limit.

After finding a parking space not far from the shrubs, she got out and began to gather the dark, shiny hollylike leaves. A squadron of girls in shorts and sweat shirts who came marching out of the west entrance to the coliseum distracted her for a few moments. Fussed at by a short, extremely pretty woman with stiff lacquered hair, the girls began twirling their fake rifles to a disco beat that blared from a loudspeaker near the yaupon bushes. Watching them—the high stepping, the rampant gum chewing, the mistakes (a rifle soared away from a tall redhead with a bland look on her face)—Donna Lee suddenly felt like crying. How tired she was of being alone! How nice it would be to pick up a Styrofoam rifle and twirl it in time to the music!

The pockets of her ancient raccoon coat filled with leaves, Donna Lee went back to the parking lot with a heavy heart. A van carrying a Brahma bull had pulled up next to her. She backed up slowly, the bull's bloodshot eyes peering dully at her from behind its bars, then, *thud*—she braked. Someone had run into her, a yellow car on the other side of the van. She got out and waved both arms at the driver of the car, but to her amazement he drove right past her as if nothing had happened, and pulled out of the parking lot. In profile that vacant look on the driver's face was so familiar, the mouth slightly ajar; she ran her hand over the dent in the Volvo, trying to recall the face. The dent wasn't so bad, but still it was a dent. Shading her eyes, she looked to see where the yellow car might have gone, but there was no sign of it. Of course—it was Pickens. Only he could hit someone in broad daylight and be totally unaware of it. The stench from the bull's van drove her away from contemplating the dent any longer. She got back inside the car.

Back in Tula Springs Donna Lee went straight to her apartment and fixed herself a martini. Although she had lived there for almost a year, the apartment looked as if she had just moved in. A box filled with extra linens, seashells, and old letters from friends sat on the couch she was planning to re-upholster. On the tacky linoleum that covered perfectly wonderful oak-block flooring was a brass wall lamp, which she didn't want to screw in until she removed the "contemporary design" wallpaper that her father had installed while she was visiting a girl friend in New York. *Totem and Taboo* provided the fourth leg to the armchair Donna Lee had found at the city dump. It was a very comfortable chair, clean as could be, but Mrs. Keely refused to set foot in the apartment until it was removed. Donna Lee flopped into the chair and tried to read.

After a second martini Donna Lee climbed down the rickety wooden stairs outside her apartment to examine the dent in the Volvo again. She hated to think of herself as being so middle class that a dent upset her. On the way home from Ozone she had convinced herself that it really didn't matter. After all, a car was for getting from one place to another. It was not—as so many American men felt—an extension of your personality. Besides, she'd rather not get involved with Mr. Pickens. He was a pain in the neck.

Taking a few steps back for a critical look at the car—she had bought it in 1979, the year her mother's father died, leaving Donna Lee a healthy trust fund—she suddenly realized that all her excuses for not confronting Mr. Pickens added up to this simple fact: She was a marshmallow. "Dammit!" she cried, kicking the tire. Why hadn't she charged Pickens for the office visit? And now, just because that damn urban planner was making her feel worthless, was she going to allow Pickens to walk all over her again? No, ma'am, she wasn't.

The phone book was not by the phone. She thought she remembered seeing it in the refrigerator, which alarmed her a little, until she realized the memory was of a recent dream. Just as she was about to dial information the phone rang.

"Donna Lee"—it was her mother—"I just wanted to inform you that I'm taking an incomplete in abnormal psychology. I've reached my limit with it and refuse to hear another word Mr. Hale has to say about it."

"Okay, fine with me."

"I can't understand why you made me take it in the first place."

"Because, Mother, I thought it was high time you learned something about real life. You've had your head buried in the sand for too long. By the way, would you mind looking up a number for me?"

"Is it any wonder, baby, why you go around with such a long face? How can anyone bear to live, knowing such things go on? I was thinking about it just yesterday at that nice new student union at St. Jude—they have the best cinnamon rolls there—and do you know what happened? I started crying. I just couldn't stand the thought that your father's head was filled with abnormal thoughts—because that's what Mr. Hale told us. He said that everyone normal was really abnormal underneath it all."

"It's not just Dad. It's you too, Mother."

"Then I must not be normal. Because, dear child, I *assure* you, I've never had an abnormal thought in my life."

"Of course. Now would you please look up Pickens in the phone book for me?"

Something clattered to the floor on the other end of the line.

Mrs. Keely groaned, then bumped the receiver against the wall. "Moab, go outside and tell Mr. Keely he'll have to take off his pants and shoes before coming inside. I won't have him trailing mulch over my waxed floor. Look at him, there's mulch all over him. Donna Lee, what was that again?"

"Pickens, Bobby Pickens."

"Hmm. There's no Bobby. Louella—you want Louella? And a Carl R. They're both at Five-seventeen Sweetgum."

"Five-seventeen Sweetgum."

"The number is eight, four . . . Who is this Pickens? You know, Donna Lee, the boy should always call the girl. I don't care how modern you are, the boy should *always* call the girl."

"This is business."

"Even so, there are standards."

"Good-bye, Mother."

"Listen, baby, I haven't time to gab with you now, sorry. Thank you for calling." Mrs. Keely hung up.

Donna Lee decided she had had enough of phones. Sweetgum was the next street over; she would take the shortcut and pay Mr. Pickens a personal call.

Walking past the car, she ran her hand over a persimmon tree's tough old hide, warty as an alligator's; then, after stepping over knee-high palmettos, she cut around the unsightly hole that would one day be the pool that would raise everyone's rent. Donna Lee lived in the old, unrenovated section of the Hollywood Apartments, where, for some reason, she sometimes got a slight electric shock when she took a shower. Mr. Herbert advised her not to sue her landlord, who had told Donna Lee, after testing the shower, that it wasn't the plumbing needed fixing, it was her head. So, begrudgingly Donna Lee gave up showers and stuck to baths.

The ditch in back, choked by water lettuce, had a lichened plank thrown across it. Donna Lee crossed here and ended up in someone's backyard. Although it was cold for November, the false garlic and milkweed looked hearty amid the dying St. Augustine. Hugging her raccoon coat to her, she hurried along the cane hedge, observing as she went that the narrow frame house whose backyard she was using as a shortcut sagged a little on one of its brick pilings. When she was five, Donna Lee had crawled under a house like this and tried to set fire to it. There was no malice in her heart, simply curiosity. The cobwebbed cypress beams were too damp, though, and she ran out of matches.

There were no numbers on the front door of this narrow little house. She walked next door to a brick house and saw it was 777, which didn't make much sense, since Dr. Henry's, which was on the same side of the street and only one house away, was 124. She went back to the numberless house, climbed three concrete steps to the front porch, and rang the doorbell.

A man answered, dripping wet, with a towel around his waist.

"I'm very sorry," Donna Lee said, suddenly wishing she had chewed some Clorets; her breath must reek from the martinis. "Is this Five-seventeen Sweetgum?"

The muscles in the man's brown chest—big, disgusting muscles—rippled; his eyebrows went up. "Let's see," he said, poking his head out the door and peering at the doorframe above the mailbox. "Don't know, lady. It doesn't say."

"Well, is this the home of Bobby Pickens?"

The man shrugged. "I've seen someone looks like him wander in and out occasionally."

"Is he here now? I'd like to speak to him." Donna Lee tried to sound severe, but her tongue was thick and slow.

"You a friend or something?"

"He ran into me today, put a big dent in my Volvo."

"You sure it was him?" His black eyes looked blurred, unfocused.

"Yes, of course. He ran into me and then just drove away like nothing happened."

The man's jaws started working, as if he had a wad of gum inside. "That's him, all right, out to lunch. Well, like you know, I'm sort of freezing to death."

"Would you tell him—"

"Where'd he run into you? In town here?"

"Ozone. St. Jude, really."

He sniffed, then sniffed again, dancing from one foot to the other. Donna Lee recognized the sniff, and it had nothing to do with colds. This man was a cokehead.

"Well, bye and all that sort of thing," he said, giving her a big wink.

"You tell him I—"

"Yeah, right, I got you, babe—dent, Volvo, everyone pissed off . . ." The door shut.

She stood there a moment, her fists clenched, then turned and went down the steps.

CHAPTER

Eighteen

After Burma told him about F.X.'s plan, Mr. Pickens knew no peace. Strange noises obsessed him; he had to know what every sound meant. When he came home, each and every closet had to be inspected; then, before going to sleep, he would poke under his bed with a broom.

One day F.X. got a runny nose and started acting real palsy-

walsy. He laughed at anything Mr. Pickens said, slapping him
on the back, complimenting him, all the time pacing around
the house, jittery as a june bug. Mr. Pickens was sure this was
it; the plan was going to happen. That night, after being on
guard all day, he arranged pillows and cushions under his
blankets to look like himself, then sat by the bedroom's open
window, prepared to flee at the sound of a creaking floorboard,
a whisper, or the three notes of the door chimes.

A few minutes later he awoke in mid-snore when a car back-
fired in Dr. Henry's parking lot. The first thing he saw in the
night-light's dim glow was himself lying asleep on his bed. It
was a terrible shock. Right then and there he decided he
couldn't take it any longer. So, after leaving F.X. a note saying
he had gone to Tucson to visit his father, Mr. Pickens ran
away from home.

Of course he had no intention of going to Tucson for a visit
with someone who was incommunicado. Besides, it was too
long a trip, too expensive. The main thing was to get out of
sight so F.X. couldn't use him in his damn-fool plan to become
a celebrity. That night he drove south to Ozone and checked
into the Pontchartrain Courts, a motel whose sole charm de-
rived from the fact that Toinette had slept there once. The
next day he went to the parish courthouse and found out that
the title deed to 517 Sweetgum was listed in his father's name.
Depressed by this news, he wondered if he should have a talk
with Mike, F.X.'s parole officer. But he hated getting mixed up
with the law, especially when he didn't have any hard evidence
against F.X. Indeed it was F.X. who had the hard evidence
against him. So Mr. Pickens went to the Chamber of Commerce
to see if they had a brochure on interesting sights to visit in
Ozone—monuments, old homes, Civil War battlefields, stuff
like that. They didn't. He went back to the motel for a nap.

In the morning he drove across the causeway to New Orleans, where he got lost in a mean-looking neighborhood while trying to find the Audubon Park Zoo. Later that day, back on the North Shore, as he was inquiring about tickets to cultural events on the St. Jude campus, he happened to see a familiar face among the Fighting Otters Marching Corps. It was Toinette. He watched her from a distance until the girls filed back into the coliseum. The next day, armed with field binoculars he had bought at Sears, he sat in the parking lot of the coliseum, watching and dreaming. He had brought along a Thermos of bourbon and Tab, Toinette's drink, to help soothe the ache in his heart. Once, when the rifle she was twirling flew out of her hands, he yanked open the car door, prepared to run headlong across the practice field to fetch it for her. But, thinking of the consequences, he stopped himself, slammed the door, and finished off the Thermos.

Lying on the vibrating motel bed that evening, Mr. Pickens couldn't get Toinette out of his mind—those incredibly long legs, the semaphoring arms, her blue short shorts, that white rifle. It was too dangerous. He knew if he stayed in Ozone, he would be doing all his sight-seeing at the St. Jude coliseum. Imagine if someone caught him—drunk, binoculared, looking like a common pervert. And worse: He knew if he kept watching, one day he would not be able to resist running across that field and declaring himself to her. Then what? F.X., the stolen watch, police, indictments, fingerprints, courtrooms . . .

When Mr. Pickens had first run away from home, Burma, who was the only one he confided in now, suggested that he come live with her and Emmet. Her mother was away in Cairo, Illinois, visiting a sister whose daughter had just got secretly married to an Indian from India. Mr. Pickens had turned down the invitation, politely but firmly. He could not imagine anything he'd like less than living with Burma and Emmet. But now, besides Toinette worries, he had money worries. After next week there would be no more unemployment compensation.

The vibrating bed stopped jiggling. Mr. Pickens sighed and put another quarter into the coin box on the headboard. Then he picked up the phone to make a long distance call to Tula Springs.

Except for Emmet life wasn't so bad at the LaSteele house. Burma came home every noon from Sonny Boy and made lunch for Mr. Pickens, then did the dishes while he took a nap. Emmet, though, was another story. For starters he decided that now that Mrs. LaSteele was gone, he wouldn't wear clothes around the house. Burma was too weak and discouraged from her diet to offer much protest, so Mr. Pickens had to put up with the sight of Emmet in his T-shirt and briefs. Emmet had a long pink scar on his dark leg that Mr. Pickens had to try hard not to stare at. It came from the same jeep accident that put a ton of glass in Emmet's face. The face was eventually reconstructed after nine operations, which the U.S. Army paid for. The Army also sent him a check every month because of the accident, which wasn't Emmet's fault.

Another thing about Emmet—he was addicted to dirty magazines. When Mrs. LaSteele was around, he hid them inside the broken Hammond organ in the living room. But while Burma's mother was in Cairo the magazines were strewn about everywhere. Mr. Pickens asked Burma if they didn't bother her. She said they did but that Emmet had promised to get rid of them once they got married. The magazines made it very hard for Mr. Pickens to think straight, especially when he was alone.

Stretched out on Mrs. LaSteele's heart-shaped bed, Mr. Pickens, who had been installed at Burma's for a week now and was feeling quite at home, perused the local paper's society column, known as "Mrs. Jenks at Large." Eleven years ago

Mr. Pickens had made the column when he poured for a tea his mother gave at the Baptist Church's Kingdom Hall. He kept on hoping his name would be mentioned again ("Seen at the opening night of the opera at St. Jude Saturday night was Tula Springs' own man-about-town, MR. CARL ROBERT PICKENS, wearing a stunning ensemble from Fraternity Row"), but it never was.

"She says she hates college," Burma said, "but at least her feet don't hurt so much." She was sitting on a pink organdy-skirted chair, which, like all the other furniture in the house, seemed a little too small for adult human beings. Mr. Pickens's feet hung over the edge of the bed, and he wasn't tall at all.

"What about F.X.? Did she say anything about F.X.?"

Burma shrugged. She still had on her green Sonny Boy uniform, which was made out of a plasticlike material that was supposed to repel dirt. Burma wore it around the house because it made her sweat a lot; she wanted to melt inches away, like they said on the TV commercials for those reducing belts.

"Well?"

"Oh, please don't snap at me, Bobby Pickens. My head is spinning from that diet pill I just took."

"This is important. I got to know."

Burma rubbed a grimy hand against her forehead. "You're going to get mad if I tell you."

"Tell me what?"

"Well, somehow F.X. knows you haven't gone off to Tucson. He knows you're around."

Mr. Pickens's pale eyes went dim. "You blabbed. You blabbed to Toinette. I just knew this would happen."

"Now, look here—"

"You betrayed me," he said quietly, solemnly, "you betrayed me with those great big fat lips of yours." With a sigh of resignation he folded his hands over his chest. The news-

paper shrouded the white bare legs that stuck out from his
paisley bathrobe.

"That does it!" Burma's hand banged down on the dressing
table, upsetting several bottles of nail polish. "Just because
you got cancer don't give you no right to talk to me like that.
No, sir!"

Mr. Pickens's head, sunk deep in the pillow, turned slowly
toward her. There was a stricken look on his round boyish
face that made Burma put her hand over her mouth.

"Oh, Bobby," she said in a small voice, "I'm sorry, I'm so
sorry. I swore I'd never let on I knew you were sick and all. I
could kill myself, really I could." Tears welled up in her eyes.
A black line streaked down her cheek.

"How did you know?" he asked.

"The receptionist in Dr. McFlug's office, Honey Baker, she's
a friend of this friend of mine. I've known all along, but she
said I couldn't let on I knew, 'cause Dr. McFlug would fire her
if he thought she was gossiping. Anyway, I mean, that's why I
wanted you to be best man at my wedding. I thought it'd give
you something to look forward to, something to help you forget all your troubles. See, I— What do you want, Emmet?"

Emmet had stuck his head into the room. "Nothing," he
said with a blank look on his sharp, rodentlike face. His body
was small, wizened, as if he had a history of malnutrition.

"Well?" Burma said peevishly.

"What are y'all doing?" he asked, poking his head in the
doorway a little farther. The bamboo wind chimes above the
door tinkled lightly.

"Why don't you go practice?" Burma asked. "How come I
never hear you tootin' that clarinet?"

"Mr. Pickens don't take to it."

"I never said such a thing," Mr. Pickens said, yanking a
loose bead off his moccasin slippers.

"Look, Burma," Mr. Pickens said once Emmet had wandered off into the other room, "as you well know, I don't have that cancer anymore."

"You don't?"

"That's right. I'm not dying."

Burma scratched her head, ruining the part in her pageboy hairstyle. "Oh," she said.

"Oh?"

"I mean good, that's real good."

"You don't sound very happy about it."

She looked doubtfully at her bitten nails. "Well, to tell you the truth, I just don't see how—"

"Didn't that dang friend of yours tell you? The lab made a mistake. There was a mix-up with the computer."

"Well, I never seen Honey again. See, she's really not that good a friend. Like I told you, she's a friend of a friend."

Mr. Pickens sat up and tossed the paper on the floor. "Did you tell Emmet I was dying?"

"I had to, Bobby. How else could I explain why you were coming here to live while Mama was away?"

"I told you to tell him that I quit my job and can't afford my rent for now."

"I did. I said all that. But somehow it didn't seem enough for Emmet. I needed some more reasons." Burma peered into the dressing table mirror but didn't seem to see the mascara on her cheeks. "You know, I feel sort of funny. If you're not really sick . . . I mean, I thought . . ."

"What do you want me to do?"

"I don't know. Except maybe you could, well, you know . . ."

She did not finish, but Mr. Pickens knew what she meant to say. She wanted him to go back and tell F.X. he knew about the plan and he didn't care if F.X. got him arrested for stealing the watch or not—he was not going to let F.X. get away with ruining Toinette's life. Nevertheless, as Mr. Pickens had explained to Burma time and time again, it wasn't fair that forty-one years of morality should go down the drain all because of one stupid watch. He was innocent, and that was that.

"Listen, Burma, if you think this is easy, lying here all day long . . ." Since Sweetgum was only a few blocks from Mrs. LaSteele's house, Mr. Pickens was afraid to go out in the yard, much less go to a movie or Baskin-Robbins. He kept his car in the garage with the garage door shut twenty-four hours a day. "Okay, maybe I'm not dying, but that doesn't mean I'm not suffering."

"Oh, please, you're not going to start on that again. If you really loved Toinette like you say, you'd stop mooning around and stand up to F.X. Now, when you was sick, Carl Robert, that was a different story. *Then* I could understand how the strain might be too much. I wanted to protect you from that stinking brother of yours and—"

"I'm sorry, Burma. But to me Truth is more important. If you don't have Truth, then nothing matters—not Love, not Loyalty, not Friendship."

"What truth you talking about?"

"My Innocence. I will not let myself be accused of something I did not do. I did not steal that watch."

Burma stared at him dully. There were dark circles under her eyes, and her feet were swollen in her rubber-soled shoes. With a sigh she leaned over and undid the laces, noticing as she did so the stack of wedding invitations on the pink shag carpet.

"This all you done today?" she asked, picking up a handful of envelopes. As a favor Mr. Pickens had volunteered to address the wedding invitations for her.

"I've been thinking real hard today," Mr. Pickens replied a little defensively.

"Thinking?"

"About my career. I decided the restaurant business wasn't for me, and neither was insurance, like I told you about the other day. See, Burma, to be in business, any sort of business, you can't have too many scruples, too many ethics. That's always been my problem. I've never got ahead in the business world for one reason: I'm too moral." He paused to let this sink in. "There's some people like me who God's weighed down with a heavy burden of morality, a real penetrating sense of right and wrong. We just can't escape it no matter how hard we try. Now think a minute, Burma, what sort of career would that fit into?"

"I don't know. A lawyer?"

He gave her a stern look. "Preacher, Burma. Preacher. It just struck me today: All along, why I've felt so depressed and everything, why, that's God's way of calling me. I have a calling. That's why He saved me from cancer, so I could answer that calling."

In fact Mr. Pickens had convinced himself that if he devoted himself to God, God would reciprocate by either making Toinette fall in love with him or making him fall out of love with her—he didn't care which, just so long as one of them happened soon. The pain of love denied was wearing him down, especially now that this love had got all tangled up with F.X. and thievery and perjury and everything illegal he could think of.

"Bobby, you're too old to start being a preacher," she said peevishly.

"Who says?"

"What about college? You admitted to me just yesterday you never finished."

"Did Jesus go to college? Did Matthew, Mark, Luke, or John?"

"Brother Washburn did."

Mr. Pickens shook his head slowly, emphatically. "You know what's wrong with you? You're a negative thinker. You always think negative. That's why you've never got anywhere in life. That's why you still work in a run-down dump of a store and wear all that eye shadow."

"Was it *you* studied makeup at the beauty college, or me?"

"I can't help saying the Truth, Burma. Believe me, it'd be much easier to just pretend there was nothing wrong with the way you put on makeup. Now, don't start crying. You said yourself the other night that I should be honest with you, remember?"

She plucked a Kleenex from its designer box.

"All right," he said, holding up both hands, "if you'd rather I wasn't honest, fine."

"Why is it you're the one always gets to be honest?" she said. "I'd like to be honest back once in a while."

"Go right ahead. Who's stopping you?"

"You, that's who. Just last night I was trying to tell you how I felt about you and—"

"Shhh!" He pointed to the door.

"Don't shush me. Emmet can hear if he likes. I'm not saying anything wrong. Oh, Lord, Bobby, you get me so confused. I mean, ever since you come here I've felt we've been growing so close, in a pure way, like a brother and sister, sort of plutonic, you know. I sometimes think I never felt so close to a man before. But then all of a sudden you come out with some crack like that one you made about my makeup. How do you think that makes me feel? I mean, what if I told you I didn't like your double chin?"

"What double chin?" Mr. Pickens palped his chin, alarmed.

From the living room came the sound of Mrs. LaSteele's

Hammond organ, which could only play the black notes; as a result everything played on it sounded Chinese.

"Emmet, shut the heck up!" Burma called out. She hated Oriental music; it made her think of slimy things.

"I don't have a double chin," Mr. Pickens said.

Emmet's head appeared in the doorway again. "Can I have some okra?"

"Not until you put some clothes on," Mr. Pickens said.

"I swear," Burma said at the same time, "you must got a tapeworm, Emmet. Three bowls of Cool Whip for dessert, now you want okra."

"Put some clothes on."

"Oh, hush, Bobby," Burma said, getting up from the chair. "Come on, Emmet. I'll get you your okra."

CHAPTER

Nineteen

"What are we looking for?" Donna Lee asked. She and her mother and father were trailing behind Moab as the old woman combed the aisles of a vast drugstore on the mall's second level. Donna Lee had driven everyone to Mississippi this evening after work since Mrs. Keely's Datsun was at the repair shop. Mrs. Keely insisted she smelled smoke every time she drove it, a peculiar scented type of smoke, almost like burnt apricots. Mr. Keely's Olds 98 was on loan to Dr. McFlug, who was getting his Lincoln repainted a darker shade of beige to save on car-wash bills.

"Don't be so impatient," Mrs. Keely said to Donna Lee, as

they all paused in front of a rack of hairbrushes. Moab peered skeptically at the brushes.

"By the way," Mrs. Keely said to her daughter, "Mrs. Jenks was talking about her handyman today, Mr. Ray. He has a swollen heart, that's why he can't eat. So really, baby, you must stop saying she's starving him. She bends over backwards trying to get him to eat, but he won't. It's too painful."

"A swollen heart?" Donna Lee frowned.

"He's rheumatic or something. She says the heart pumped up too big, overcompensating for a valve or something, and it started pressing against his food tube. I never really knew, but Mrs. Jenks said the heart was really nothing but a muscle, a great big muscle, and if it gets exercised too much, it can swell up just like a weight lifter's biceps. You've seen those weight lifters, how huge their muscles get. Dad, put that brush down."

"Sounds weird to me."

"That's exactly what she told Babette."

"Babette?"

"The operator who was doing her hair. Mrs. Jenks was in the next booth—she didn't know I was on the other side of the partition with Sherlene. Anyway, that's not all Mrs. Jenks said. She said Tula Springs was full of atheists, and she started to name a few. I had to put my hands over my ears when she got to you. I just didn't want to hear any more."

Moab headed for the next aisle. Everyone followed.

"You have your father to thank for that," Mrs. Keely said, eyeing some tweezers. "Dr. McFlug has told everyone you don't believe in God."

"Of all the—"

"Well, you don't, do you?"

"Not in *his* God, not in Mrs. Jenks's God. I have my own God."

The Muzak was interrupted by an announcement that there was a two-for-one sale on vitamins C and E on aisle 16. Moab glared at the loudspeaker, then went back to examining some spools of thread. She was a tiny woman with smooth, tight coffee-colored skin and sparse reddish hair. She wore a varsity football sweater from Tula Springs High—it reached below her knees—and spotless Adidas jogging shoes, which she polished once a week. Donna Lee was a little afraid of Moab, who hadn't spoken a word to her since she started working for the Keelys about a year ago. This seemed unfair to Donna Lee, especially since she had tried many times to start up a real conversation with her, not, like her mother, just gab about petty household matters. Moab's silence hurt Donna Lee and made her wonder about herself.

"Moab, that's a nice color. Why don't you buy that?" Mrs. Keely said.

"Ugly," Moab said with a look of disgust, and walked on.

"Did I tell you, baby," Mrs. Keely said, turning to her daughter, "I heard Mrs. Jenks ask Babette if Donna Lee Keely was married." Mr. Keely stumbled into a bin of shampoo. Stores disoriented him; he was always looking at signs and mirrors rather than where he was going. Mrs. Keely yanked him by the sleeve and told him to behave, then went on to Donna Lee: "Babette said she thought you were married."

"Why didn't you tell them the truth?" Donna Lee asked. Her legs ached like an old woman's. She really was terribly out of shape. In New Orleans she used to jog all the time in Audubon Park, but when she tried jogging in Tula Springs, a grizzled farmer with a wad of tobacco in his cheek offered to give her a lift in the back of his pickup, then she got chased by a mangy three-legged dog.

"Donna Lee, I'm not the sort of woman who butts into other

people's conversations. Besides, I'd rather they thought you *were* married. I'm just so tired of explaining to people why you aren't."

"Explaining? Mother, it's none of their damn business. And what do you mean, explain? What do you say?"

"I tell them the truth. I tell them you haven't found yourself yet. Once you've come to your senses, then you'll start accepting dates with nice boys like Dr. Elridge's brother."

"He's a dentist. Do you want me to end up the wife of a dentist?"

"Mrs. Elridge is the wife of a dentist. She's got a gorgeous home, all the clothes she could want, friends galore. Really, baby, you are a snob. Dr. Elridge's brother is so nice, such a good sense of humor. But no, you won't be content till you've married the king of Siam." She sighed, unclasped her alligator purse, then snapped it shut. "It's that urban planner's fault. I knew the minute I met him he was no good. Just too handsome, that's all. I don't trust men that are that handsome. Oh, good heavens, now where did Moab go? Leon, why didn't you keep an eye on her?"

When Donna Lee got back to her apartment that evening, she thought about going jogging, then fixed herself a martini in a jelly glass instead. But she couldn't enjoy it. The neighbors next door had started a row. "Where's the Downy!" the husband screamed. "What the fuck's a Downy!" the wife screamed back. "Fucking fabric softener!" Donna Lee rapped on the wall with her jogging shoe, and the brass wall lamp she had installed that morning plummeted to the floor. She stooped and switched it off.

After finishing the martini Donna Lee decided to jog over to Sweetgum to see if Mr. Pickens was home. Her father had noticed the dent in the Volvo in the parking lot of the mall, and Donna Lee resolved once again that Mr. Pickens wasn't going to get away with it. While changing into sweat pants and a sweat shirt she finished another martini as ammunition against the cold.

There was no moon. Gingerly she made her way around the hole in back of the Hollywood Apartments until her eyes adjusted to the dark. Jogging along the ditch, she looked for the plank that led to Mr. Pickens's backyard. She had planned to run the long way around, which was about a half mile, but once she was outside her apartment she realized it was too cold for that.

The plank was at a funny angle, so she tested it with one foot; it wobbled. She stood there a moment, hugging herself. If only the ditch were a hundred feet deep, not just five or six, then she would use that damn plank, lose her footing accidentally, and be done with it. She was so tired, so fucking tired. Everything seemed to exhaust her, not just the work she did at Mr. Herbert's, but even the little things, like taking her parents to the mall.

A door creaked in one of the apartments behind her. She realized she couldn't just stand there; it looked too suspicious. Neither could she balance across the plank with all the gin in her. So, crouching first, she leapt, grabbing a tree limb when she hit the other side. A dog started yapping. Donna Lee hurried along the cane hedge that separated Mr. Pickens's yard from Dr. Henry's parking lot. When she got to the front of the house, she stumbled on a porch step and cursed herself.

Her breath coming hard, she gave herself a moment to recover before ringing the bell. It was then that she noticed the beam of light through the window, a single beam darting up a wall, over a mantel. The whole house was dark except for that thin strip of light.

"Hey!" Donna Lee pounded on the door with her fist.

She heard a thump, then a crash—a vase breaking, a lamp? Ringing the bell, she tried the door to see if it was open, then ran as fast as she could around the side of the house to the back.

"Stop!" she cried as the prowler rushed out the screen door in back and headed across the yard. Donna Lee was gaining on him—"Come back here, you!"—when it occurred to her what she was doing. It was too dark to see well, but he did look big. Her heart swelled up, filling her whole chest, which seemed ready to explode.

He had run behind the tool shed. Keeping her eyes fixed on the shed, Donna Lee began to retreat, planning to burrow through the cane hedge and get help at Dr. Henry's. But what was happening to her legs? They felt leaden, stricken with a dreamlike paralysis. How utterly stupid it would be to get beat up, killed, mauled while trying to defend that bloated ape's house. It just wasn't fair.

"Mommy, you said."

"Get in this car."

The voices came from the parking lot on the other side of the sugarcane. Crouched near a garbage can, Donna Lee wondered if she should scream for help.

"Are you going to get in this car, young man, or am I going to have to tan your hide?"

The scream ripped out. But it wasn't Donna Lee's.

CHAPTER

Twenty

"Can I talk to you, Mr. Pickens?"

Mr. Pickens sighed. He had the Bible open to Psalm 35, which seemed to have been written especially for him: *"I behaved myself as though he had been my friend or brother: I bowed down heavily, as one that mourneth for his mother,"* he had read, feeling extremely holy. *"False witnesses did rise up; they laid to my charge things that I knew not. . . . The abjects gathered themselves together against me."* Then, after rereading the best part (*"Let destruction come upon him at unawares; and let his net that he hath hid catch himself"*), one of the abjects wandered into the bedroom dripping Eskimo Pie onto the rug. Emmet was wearing only a pair of cotton briefs, no T-shirt this time, so that Mr. Pickens could see every rib sticking out of his leathery hide. He was bony as a gar.

"I just wanted to ask you—"

"Emmet," Mr. Pickens said in a firm yet patient voice while adjusting one of Mrs. LaSteele's pillows, an oblong one with a bear and a geyser on it. The valentine bed on which he lay had all sorts of novelty pillows, which Mrs. LaSteele collected on her vacations to the parks in the National Park System. "Emmet, I can't understand a word you're saying. Speak up. Enunciate."

Emmet was still a little shy with Mr. Pickens, not because Mr. Pickens was dying—Emmet was used to that by now; he

only hoped it didn't happen while he was looking at him—
but because Mr. Pickens's English was so good. When he had
told Mr. Pickens this the other day, Mr. Pickens decided
Emmet might be someone he could practice his preaching on.
Mr. Pickens knew that once he got his preaching diploma, he
would open a church for modern Baptists, Baptists who were
sick to death of hell and sin being stuffed down their gullets
every Sunday. There wasn't going to be any of that old-
fashioned ranting and raving in Mr. Pickens's church. *His*
Baptist church would be guided by reason and logic. Everyone could drink in moderation. Everyone could dance and pet
as long as they were fifteen—well, maybe sixteen or seventeen.
At thirty, if you still weren't married, you could sleep with
someone, and it wouldn't be a sin—that is, as long as you
loved that person. If you hit forty and were still single, you'd
be eligible for adultery not being a sin, as long as no children's
feelings got hurt and it was kept very discreet. But you still
had to love and respect the person; you couldn't just do it for
sex.

Emmet cleared his throat and fiddled with the tail of a
stuffed parrot, on which Mrs. LaSteele hung her less expensive
jewelry. "I don't know what's the matter with me, Mr. Pickens."

Mr. Pickens thought he could tell him one or two things, but
he kept his mouth shut and made a steeple of his hands, as
Brother Washburn did when he was in the pulpit.

Emmet scratched the pink scar on his leg. "It's these urge
things I got, sir. They won't leave me alone."

"I assume by 'urge things' you are referring, in a colloquial
sense, to sexual matters."

Emmet nodded, looking very solemn. Mr. Pickens wished
he could come right out and tell Emmet he wasn't dying, so
everyone could act more natural, but Burma didn't think this
would be such a good idea. It was strange how things were

working out with Burma. They behaved like an old married couple who weren't in love anymore. The domesticity of their life was a comfort to Mr. Pickens, who was even learning to regard Emmet with a dim but earnest affection.

"Listen, Emmet, please don't look so lugubrious," Mr. Pickens said, anxious to try out the new word he had learned in the Word Power section of the *Reader's Digest*. "There's no call for lugubriousness."

"Sorry, sir." He tossed the wrapper of his Eskimo Pie into a flowered wastepaper basket.

"You know, Mr. Pickens, I love Burma and all that sort of thing. I'm just scared that after we get ourselves hitched, these urge things won't go away. She says she ever catches me straying, she'll scratch my eyes out."

"First of all, move that vase away from your elbow."

Emmet was sitting at the dressing table next to the bed. A glass vase of paper daffodils looked ready to slide off onto the rug. Emmet pushed the flowers away from the edge.

"Now," Mr. Pickens said, "go on, son."

"Every time I see a girl, I get the urge thing. Like just walking down the hall in the music building at St. Jude, these piano majors come by—they ain't even that pretty, not half as pretty as Burma—but still it happens. I can't think of but one thing day and night. I mean, Burma's just great in the sack, but then she goes off to work, and I'm at school and . . . well, I done lapsed three times this week. Not with the piano majors—they're too snobby. See, there's this—"

Mr. Pickens snapped the Bible shut. He did not want to hear the sordid details, so he assumed a lofty expression as he buttoned the top button of his polka-dot pajamas. "This is probably just a phase you're going through, Emmet. Soon as you hit thirty—"

"I done hit thirty already. I done hit thirty-five. See, I was in the Army ten years 'fore I went on to college. I couldn't make up my mind what to do, so I stayed on in the Army all that time. It was only when I had that jeep accident, when I was flying headfirst through that windshield, that I decided it might be fun to play the clarinet. That's what was flashing through my head, a great big clarinet, then everything went black."

"Hmmm . . ." Mr. Pickens was deep in thought. "Ah, yes," he said finally. "Polygamy. You're suffering from polygamy."

"The doctor said it was a concussion."

"No, Emmet. I'm referring to your sexual constitution. Polygamy is a sexual disorder that afflicts a tiny percentage of the adult male population. It was more common in ancient days, especially in hot climates, but evolution has weeded it out as we've evolved into more civilized types of people. By the way, you do believe in evolution, don't you?"

Emmet shrugged.

"Now, Emmet, don't look so lugubrious. I myself have someone near to me, a brother in fact, whom I suspect is afflicted with the same disorder."

"Is there something I can do? The wedding's next month."

"There's only one thing you can do, son. That's pray. Pray for the grace to resist temptation, to become a normal man again. You nod. You're saying to yourself, 'Sure, prayer, lot of good that'll do.' You can't fool me, Emmet Orney. I know the minute you leave this room you'll forget all about my advice, right? Right. Oh, maybe your conscience will give a twinge or two in the next couple days, but will you ever actually get down on your knees, get down on those two knees of yours and pray, pray for all you're worth?" Mr. Pickens smiled. "I doubt it. I doubt it very much. That's why I'm going to ask you to pray with me right now, that's right, right here and now. As they say, there's no time like the present. So do yourself a favor, Emmet, a big favor. Get down on those knees. You don't have to say a word, I'll pray for you. All I want you to do is get down on those knees."

"Couldn't I pray sitting up?"

"Knees, Emmet. Knees."

"I can't pray except when it's dark."

"All right, then, turn out the lights."

"Well . . . maybe later, huh? I got to practice, then—"

"Enunciate."

"I think maybe—"

"Turn out the lights, Emmet. Then get on your knees. This will only take a minute. And don't slouch like that. Do you think God likes to look down on a slouch?"

Emmet switched off the lamp on the dressing table while Mr. Pickens turned off the light over Mrs. LaSteele's bed.

"Are you on your knees?" Mr. Pickens asked, adjusting the pillow behind his head.

"Uh . . ." Something clattered onto the glass top of the dressing table. "Mr. Pickens, I think I spilled something."

"Never mind. O God, in Whom we trust . . ."

"It smells something awful."

"Emmet, silence."

"It's soaking into me, I got to . . ."

Lying flat on his back with his hands folded, Mr. Pickens prayed for patience while Emmet fidgeted about in the dark. Then suddenly a light went on, the overhead light in the ceiling.

Mr. Pickens propped himself up on his elbows.

A woman stood in the doorway to the bedroom, her hands on her hips. She was wearing slacks and a brown blouse, so it took Mr. Pickens a moment to place her. It was Mrs. Quaid, without her white cafeteria uniform.

"You," she said, staring at Mr. Pickens, who now noticed

that Emmet was standing by the bed stark naked, his briefs in his hand. A bottle of cologne lay on its side on the dressing table.

"*You,*" Mrs. Quaid repeated with such loathing that Mr. Pickens's face crumpled, as if from a blow. Emmet scooted into bed and pulled the blanket over his middle.

"God help me," Mrs. Quaid said, wringing her large chapped hands.

Dressed in his leisure suit and matching blue loafers, Mr. Pickens sat on a spindly chair in Mrs. LaSteele's tiny living room, which was so crammed with furniture and knickknacks it resembled a thrift shop. Emmet, in a plaid suit that Mr. Pickens made him put on, was sitting on the organ bench, pressing a black note tentatively every now and then. Enveloped in a cloud of cigarette smoke, Mrs. Quaid sat beneath a matador and bull painted on black velvet.

"Where is your intended?" she asked Emmet.

Emmet shrugged.

"She's at the mall in Mississippi, shopping," Mr. Pickens said. "Now, if you'd kindly explain what you're doing here, I'd . . ." The look she directed at him made him trail off.

"Please," he said more docilely as a wave of panic churned up his stomach. Perspiration covered his nose. "We were just praying, me and Emmet."

"And you better keep on praying, mister." She coughed and stubbed out her half-finished cigarette. "You want to know what I'm doing here? Fine. I'll tell you. See these?" She dangled some keys. "Hattie give me these. She wants me to check up on Burma and Emmet every now and then, make sure they turned off the gas on the stove, stuff like that. So I come. And what do I find? The door locked, the lights out. Now, you take it from there, Pickens."

"It might surprise you, Mrs. Quaid, but I just happen to reside here currently. I am the invited guest of Mrs. LaSteele's daughter. Right, Emmet?"

Emmet shrugged, his back to them.

"As for the door being locked, I always lock the door." His mouth was dry as cotton. He wished he had some water. "This is the age of crime, Mrs. Quaid. I feel responsible for protecting Mrs. LaSteele's property in this lugubrious time when no city, no town, no hamlet is immune from crime. As for the lights, that's simple. Emmet can't pray except when it's dark. In the interest of prayer he extinguished the lights."

"Hold on a sec. You say you live here?"

"Visiting."

"I see, visiting." Mrs. Quaid picked up the cigarette she had stubbed out and put it in her mouth, unlit. "You got your own house a couple blocks away, and you're visiting. Does Hattie know about this?"

"Hattie? You mean Mrs. LaSteele?"

"That's right, Mrs. LaSteele."

"Emmet," Mr. Pickens said, "does Mrs. LaSteele know I'm here? Of course she does. Would her own daughter presume otherwise?"

"How long do you plan to visit, Pickens? I'm sure Hattie would like to know so she can make arrangements to find herself another bed."

"Till he's dead," Emmet muttered.

"What's that, Emmet?" Mrs. Quaid brushed back a strand of gray hair that had strayed from her hairnet. "Look at me when you talk."

"Mr. Pickens is dying. You hadn't ought to snap at him, Miss Quaid," Emmet replied, peering over his shoulder at her. "Cancer. Cancer of the back."

"Is this true, Pickens?"

Mr. Pickens opened his mouth, then closed it, then opened it again. "In a way, yes. I was once suffering from melanoma."

Emmet swiveled around on the organ bench. "Once? You mean you ain't dying no more?"

"I tried to tell you, Emmet. I tried my best. But Burma wouldn't let me. She made me keep quiet."

Emmet glowered at the organ stops. "How'd you stop dying?"

His mind awhirl, Mr. Pickens glanced nervously at Mrs. Quaid, who was poised at the edge of her seat like she was fixing to lunge at him. "Prayer, Emmet. God's mercy and prayer."

"Lord, I don't know what either of you's jabbering about," she said, getting up. "Degenerate talk, huh? Think I won't understand. Well, I'll tell you one thing, buster." She stabbed the air with her unlit cigarette. "I'm staying right here till Burma gets home. Then I'm going to tell her everything I saw—everything. Then, mister, if she needs any help disposing of the trash lying around this house, I'm going to roll up my sleeves and help, you better believe." She started to cough violently. When she recovered, she said, "In the meantime, Emmet, you go get some water and soak that philodendron. Pickens, this rug could use a good vacuuming. When was the last time you bums vacuumed? And look at this dust. Hattie would die, just die."

Mr. Pickens hoisted himself out of the chair.

"Mercy," Mrs. Quaid said wearily as she glanced down at the sex magazines on the coffee table, "you think you've seen everything—"

"Those aren't mine," Mr. Pickens said. "I think they're disgusting and—"

"Go, go get the vacuum. I don't want to hear another peep out of you."

"But really they aren't. I tried to . . ." He wandered off into the kitchen.

CHAPTER

Twenty-one

Goose pimples covered the prowler's chubby arms, and her teeth chattered uncontrollably, yet still Donna Lee could not persuade her to come inside the apartment to warm up. They stood on the second-story landing, right outside Donna Lee's screen door, which was covered with crossvine that trailed down from an overhanging branch of the persimmon.

"You're freezing," Donna Lee said, plucking a piece of water lettuce from the prowler's soaking hair. When she had heard the scream a few minutes ago, Donna Lee had hurried across Mr. Pickens's backyard and discovered the prowler—who turned out to be a she, not a he—lying in the ditch near the rotting plank with her foot tangled in a patch of catbrier. After fishing her out, Donna Lee brought the woman, who was in tears, back to the Hollywood Apartments, assuring her along the way that there were no snakes in the ditch. It was too cold for them.

"Listen, you might as well make up your mind," Donna Lee said, her face slightly averted so the woman wouldn't smell the liquor on her breath. Donna Lee realized she had drunk far too much, and was feeling very woozy. "I'm not going to let you go home like this. You'll die of pneumonia. So come in, dry off, and I'll drive you home, okay?" She held open the screen door. "By the way, what's your name, dear?"

The woman sniffed loudly and flicked her flashlight on and off. "April," she muttered.

Donna Lee put a hand behind the suspect and propelled her indoors. Her patience was wearing thin.

After yet another tedious discussion Donna Lee finally talked the prowler into getting out of her sopping clothes and taking a nice hot shower. While the woman was in the bathroom Donna Lee made a pot of oat straw tea and arranged some cocktail crackers and saltless goat cheese on a Wedgwood plate.

In a few minutes the prowler emerged from the bathroom bundled up in Donna Lee's terrycloth robe. She was crying again, silently.

"Here, try this," Donna Lee said, thrusting a steaming mug of tea at her.

"That shower," the woman said, her round pretty face rosy with a healthy glow, "it stung me something awful."

"You mean like a shock?"

The woman nodded.

Donna Lee went to the ancient Underwood typewriter that sat on top of the rolltop desk in her living room and began to clack out a statement about the shower, which she would have the prowler sign right this minute, before Donna Lee forgot, and which Donna Lee would slip under the landlord's door first thing in the morning.

"Your last name, April," Donna Lee said, looking up from the typewriter.

"What's that?"

"I'm taking a statement about the shower, a little deposition. My landlord thinks I'm crazy; he thinks I imagine the shocks."

"I don't know," the woman said, peering over Donna Lee's shoulder. "What's that attorney stuff up there?" Donna Lee was using letterhead stationery from Mr. Herbert's.

"That's me. I'm a lawyer."

The woman blew on her tea. "Listen, miss . . ."

"Donna Lee."

"Miss Lee, you've been real nice and all, but really, I don't want to get messed up in anything legal."

"Donna Lee. Now, April, I'm afraid you're already messed up in something legal."

"Huh?"

"Dear, I caught you prowling around someone's house with a flashlight. That's breaking and entering."

"But I told you I didn't take nothing, ma'am."

"It doesn't matter. You still broke the law. Now, please, your last name."

The woman collapsed into the wing chair from the city dump. Tears rolled down her cheeks. Donna Lee reached out and patted her on the head.

"April, honey, don't worry, I'm going to help you. I told you, I'm a lawyer. But in order for me to help you, you've got to help me first. Understand?"

The woman curled her legs up under her and stared bleakly at a top-heavy pile of books stacked by the desk. "You promise nothing bad will happen to me?"

"I'll do what I can."

"What does that mean?"

"It means you're in a lot of hot water, and you better cooperate." Donna Lee looked steadily at her for a moment. "Your name, dear."

"Moses."

"Moses? *M-O-S-E-S?*"

"Yes, ma'am."

The typewriter clattered.

"Address?"

"Uh . . . Sixty-six Pine Street, Baton Rouge."

Donna Lee finished the statement, then gave the paper to April Moses. "Sign right here," she said, handing over a gold-tipped fountain pen.

Reluctantly the woman signed.

"Now can I go?" she said after Donna Lee had folded the paper and stuck it in a pigeonhole labeled NOW.

"Hon, you don't seem to understand. Just because Tula Springs doesn't have any police—"

"But you said . . ."

"I said I'd help you." Donna Lee swiveled her chair around and rolled it closer to the wing chair. "First of all, you have the right to remain silent. Anything you say may be held against you. You may—"

"Does this mean I'm under arrest?"

"What?"

"Well, that's what they always say after they arrest someone, isn't it?" She wiped her eyes with the sleeve of the robe.

"No, April, I'm your lawyer."

"If I'm not under arrest, then what do I need a lawyer for?"

"Because I might have to report you to the parish sheriff's office."

"Then how can you be my lawyer? I never heard of no lawyer turning in his own client."

Donna Lee reached for the plate of cheese and crackers. "Have some," she said, feeling a little addled. "It'll help settle you down."

Miss Moses took a handful of cheese and crammed it in her mouth. Donna Lee realized that she shouldn't have said the bit about remaining silent, but her head had started to ache, and she couldn't think straight.

"Have you ever been arrested before?"

"Ma'am? Oh, no, ma'am. Uh, do you have something I could wash this stuff down with? It's sort of dry."

"Don't you like the tea?"

"That's *tea*? Tastes more like . . . Uh, you got something cool, maybe?"

Donna Lee went into the kitchen and took a quick nip of gin to soothe her headache. Then she got a can of orange juice out of the freezer, opened the can, and spooned the concentrate into a pitcher. Three cans of water. Stir.

She brought the pitcher into the living room. "April?"

Donna Lee looked in her bedroom, in the bathroom, then went out on the landing. But there was no sign of Miss Moses. She had disappeared.

CHAPTER

Twenty-two

Mr. Pickens unscrewed the upholstery attachment to the vacuum cleaner and stuck it in its special pocket on the closet door. He felt as if he were made out of the stuff those dead, squashed stars were made out of, matter that weighed one ton per cubic inch. His heart skipped beats, his vision blurred, and the mole scar on his back itched like blazes.

"Please, Burma," he said, "let me talk."

"You got to make Miss Quaid go home," Burma pleaded. She was still wearing the terrycloth robe she had come home from the mall in. Mrs. Quaid, who had just gone into the bathroom for a moment, was very upset with her for not waiting until she had got home to try on the new robe she had bought. The idea, coming through the front door like that.

"What is she doing here, anyway?"

"Your mother gave her a set of keys. She was making a surprise spot check."

"I could kill Mama. She treats me like a fool child."

Mr. Pickens shut the closet door and rested his head against it. His breath came in shallow spurts. "Burma, now listen to me. Mrs. Quaid is going to try and tell you something, I want you to be prepared. There's not a word of truth—"

"Bobby, please, we don't have time. I'm desperate. Look at me." She grabbed a handful of the terrycloth. "Aren't you going to ask what happened?"

"You said you couldn't wait to try on the robe, you liked it so much."

"Lord, Lord, Lord," she moaned. "Do you really think I'd do something dumb as that?"

"Listen to me, Burma. I've got to tell you quick before Mrs. Quaid ruins everything. Emmet, see, can't pray unless it's dark, so—"

She dug her nails into his fleshy arms. "Bobby, I'm about to be arrested. I just run away from my lawyer, hear? I've got to hide."

"Emmet turned off the lights and . . . Arrested?"

"I got caught in your house. F.X. wasn't home, so I thought it'd be a good chance to look around. I borrowed your keys and went snooping for that watch, the watch you stole, Toinette's. I was going to steal it back from F.X. and throw it away so he wouldn't have anything to blackmail you with. Then you could tell him and his rape plan to go to hell and Toinette's life wouldn't be ruined and you could go home again and I could stop thinking about you all the time and get married in peace. I just couldn't stand worrying about F.X. no more. It was driving me bananas. I had to do something, hear? Only I got caught. Miss Lee was going to make me tell everything. I'd have to tell her you stole the watch—otherwise how could I explain what I was doing there? I got scared we might all end up in jail, you, me, Toinette."

She reached for the handkerchief in Mr. Pickens's pocket and blew her nose hard.

"How could you be so stupid?" Mr. Pickens said dully, without anger. "Don't you think I tried to get that watch back? F.X. isn't going to let it just lie around. He's got it hid, locked up good somewheres. And by the way, I did not steal it. Did *not*."

They heard Mrs. Quaid coming out of the bathroom and saying something to Emmet in the living room.

"Who was it caught you?" Mr. Pickens whispered.

"This girl, Miss Lee. Says she's a lawyer, but she sure don't act like one. A little dopey, if you know what I mean. Don't look like one neither, sort of pretty, lots of blond hair and all."

"Burma, Pickens! Y'all come on out here," Mrs. Quaid called from the living room.

"Why's your hair all wet, girl?" Mrs. Quaid demanded when they parted the beads between the kitchen and living room.

"Wet?" Burma twisted a limp strand around her finger. "Uh . . . it was raining over in Mississippi."

Mrs. Quaid looked down at Burma's pink bare feet. The toes curled. "I don't like it—no, sir, I don't like it one bit," Mrs. Quaid muttered. She cracked all the knuckles on her left hand. "Come set down next to me, Burma."

"Can't we talk later, Miss Quaid? I'm so tired."

"Set."

Burma perched on the arm of a turquoise sofa. Mr. Pickens

continued to stand, rubbing his itching back against the stucco wall.

"I want you to get yourself ready for a shock, Burma, a tremendous shock."

"Yes, ma'am."

"For starters why don't you tell me why that man—person —squirming around over there—stop that, Pickens—is living at Hattie's house here."

"He ain't dying, neither," Emmet said sullenly from the organ.

"Bobby's the best man, Miss Quaid. He's on unemployment 'cause he got fired over at Sonny Boy."

"I know. Well?"

"That's all." Burma peered over her shoulder at the drapes.

Mrs. Quaid lit a cigarette with her fancy gold lighter and inhaled deeply. "When you get right down to it, Burma, this whole tragedy could've been avoided." She directed a baleful look at Emmett's hunched-up back. "Your mother never did approve of Emmet."

"She let him live here," Burma ventured in a small voice.

"The lesser of two evils. She just didn't want you moving out of here into some seedy dump with him. Your mother's always been concerned that you come home to a clean, cheerful house every night. That's how she was raised."

"Yes, ma'am."

"It nearly killed poor Hattie when you told her you and Emmet were getting married up. But she went along with it. She thought maybe you knew what you were doing after all. You realize that's why she's in Cairo now. She's trying to adjust herself to the idea of Emmet as a son-in-law."

Everyone looked over at Emmet. Mr. Pickens had to concede that the idea of Emmet as a son-in-law might indeed take some getting used to.

"What's the matter, girl?" Mrs. Quaid asked. "Stop fidgeting."

"I'm so tired. I really need to go to bed."

"There'll be plenty of time for bed once you hear me out—believe me. Now, Burma, you know me and your mother's been best friends for years. All this time she been griping over Emmet, I been telling her to take it easy. I say to her, 'Burma's old enough to make up her own mind. If a girl don't know her own mind at thirty-seven, then she never will.' So you see, I feel personally responsible for all this mess. If it hadn't been for me, Emmet Orney wouldn't have had an ice cube's chance in hell. Hattie would've pitched him right out on his ear." Slowly, deliberately she formed a smoke ring, which everyone watched dissolve. "Now I see I've been wrong, dead wrong. And it's my unhappy chore to set matters right. Burma, there isn't going to be no wedding, not next month, not next year, never."

"What? Emmet and me's in love. Emmet, tell Miss Quaid how much you love me."

"A whole lot," he mumbled, his eyes on the newly vacuumed pink carpet.

"Burma—Emmet and Pickens, they're degenerates."

"Huh?"

"Hon, they're *serious* degenerates. I caught them both—" Mrs. Quaid blushed, then glared at Mr. Pickens. "They was breaking the law."

"Miss Quaid, what—" Burma said while a faint squeak escaped from Mr. Pickens's compressed lips.

"They're in love, Burma. Them two's in love."

"Well, good."

"Burma, you aren't catching my drift, are you, hon?"

There was a rap on the door.

"Girl, come back here," Mrs. Quaid said as Burma fled into

the hallway off the living room. "I declare," she grumbled, crossing to the door.

"Hi," a young woman said when the door opened. Mr. Pickens got up for a closer look.

"May I help you?" Mrs. Quaid asked.

It was the blond lawyer, the one in Mr. Herbert's office, Mr. Pickens saw as he sank down in the nearest chair, which turned out to be an end table. He got up and resettled himself.

"My name is Donna Lee Keely," the lawyer said, holding out her hand to Mrs. Quaid. "I'm your daughter's attorney, and I've come to return a few things to her." She was holding an A&P shopping bag in one arm.

"Lord, is there no end?" Mrs. Quaid said, motioning for the lawyer to step inside. "Is Toinette in trouble? Lord."

"Well, I hate to say anything now, but . . . Toinette? Oh, *you*," she said, seeing Mr. Pickens. "What are *you* doing here?"

"Never mind Pickens," Mrs. Quaid said. "Just tell me what's happened to my baby girl."

"Mrs. LaSteele, she left her pocketbook in my bathroom. That's how I was able to find her. And this here"—she handed her the shopping bag—"this is some of her clothes. They're a little wet."

"Mrs. Quaid," Mrs. Quaid said. "You talking about Burma, right? These are *her* clothes, not Toinette's."

"I'm sorry. Is Burma here?"

"No," Mr. Pickens said.

"I'll go get her," Mrs. Quaid said, disappearing into the next room.

"I've been looking all over for you, Mr. Pickens," the lawyer said, shedding her raccoon coat and looking doubtfully at Emmet, who was still at the organ bench, his back to the room. "Who's that?" she asked. The pink shades on Mrs. LaSteele's tasseled lamps made the lawyer's hair look synthetic, pink, like the hair on Christmas-tree angels. "And who's Mrs. Quaid?"

"I thought you were after Burma."

"So I kill two birds with one stone." She stood right over his chair. "Mr. Pickens, let's take care of you first. At three ten on November fourteenth you ran into my Volvo in the parking lot of the St. Jude coliseum. I saw you with my own two eyes. Now, sir, I insist that you pay for the cost of repairing it. Understood?"

Mr. Pickens just sat there. He was sure he had never run into her car—he had never set eyes on it before in his life—yet here she was, demanding money, making false accusations.

The lawyer's shadow fell over him. "Mr. Pickens, did you hear me?"

He buried his face in his hands. From the back room came the sound of the two women arguing.

"Mr. Pickens."

"Lawyer lady," he said quietly, his hands still covering his face, "why don't you take your little Volvo and shove it—"

"Mr. Pickens! I—"

His hands slid down to his lap, revealing a face white with determination. "You aren't getting one red cent out of Bobby Pickens, babe, not one red cent."

"I'll take you to court."

"Try, honey. Just try. 'Cause I want to tell you something. I've had it. Had it." He still spoke quietly, but there was an intense little tremolo in his voice that cowed her. Her shadow receded from his face as she went over to the sofa and sat down.

"Really," she muttered.

Emmet played a black note on the organ.

"And as for you, Miss Blab," Mr. Pickens said when Mrs. Quaid and Burma came back into the living room. He was standing now. "As for you, Miss Blabbing Lunchroom, you better watch that fat tongue of yours. You say another word about me and Emmet, and I'll—"

"You'll what?" Mrs. Quaid said, giving him a stony look. "Set down, Pickens, and stop your foolishness. Burma, blow your nose, child."

The pink-shaded lamp with the little tassels missed Mrs. Quaid's head by a mile, but she ducked anyway, as did everyone else in the room, wondering if Mr. Pickens was going to find something else to throw.

"Damn you, you abjects!" he thundered in a voice not his own. "Hellfire and tarnation!" he hollered as he jerked open the front door and went running out into the night.

CHAPTER

Twenty-three

Mr. Pickens had never felt so good in his whole life. Fury had transformed flesh into fire. He was weightless, pure energy. As he ran the two blocks to his house on Sweetgum—*his* house, goddammit!—he almost hoped someone would try to stop him. Anyone got in his way now would be knocked clear into the middle of next week.

The front door was locked. He fumbled in his pockets for his keys—where the fuck were they?—then started ramming the door with his shoulder. Not much happened as he collided with the solid oak except that an unbearable pain shot down his neck. "Christ Almighty!" he screeched, more furious than ever, and trudged off to the back door.

"F.X.!" he called out as he kicked open the screen door to the kitchen. He switched on the lights. "F.X. Pickens, you home?"

He yanked open the silverware drawer and pawed through the stainless steel knives and forks. He would find that damn watch if it was the last thing he did—he would find it and grind it up into little pieces with his bare hands. Then let F.X. try pulling any stunts in this house, his house, Bobby Pickens's house. He'd find out real quick what was what. Before F.X. could count ten, he'd be looking out from behind Angola's nice sturdy bars.

He looked under the sink. Top Job, Drāno, a dirty yellow plastic bucket, ammonia, Bon Ami, a bicycle chain. So Mrs. Quaid thought he was a fairy. Well, goddamn her to hell, he'd show her. He'd beat the living shit out of everyone, starting with F.X. That ought to teach her.

He yanked out the bicycle chain, but it pinched him badly in the tender flesh between the fingers. With a gasp he tried to let it go, but the chain bit deeper. Carefully he manipulated the teeth until he was free, then kicked the chain across the linoleum. "Take that, big man," he said, giving it another kick. "Think you're so tough. Just come on home, son, I'll take care of you."

In the living room he tore off the cushions on the love seat, on the overstuffed wing chair, and kicked over a pile of *People* and *Us* magazines. Nothing. Then in his room—his, Carl Robert Pickens's own private bedroom—he discovered something that revived his temper, which had begun to flag after so much physical exertion. F.X. had removed all Mr. Pickens's clothes from the closets and hung up his own. Even the drawers in the night table had F.X.'s things inside them, his cuff links and floss and Chap Stick. This was the limit.

Mr. Pickens yanked the carefully ironed Calvin Klein jeans

off the hangers in the closet, grabbed a few fancy cowboy shirts and a pair of lizard boots, and tossed them all out the window. Then he went to the chest of drawers. As he pulled out a handful of F.X.'s yellow bikini underwear his hand felt something hard. Opening the drawer a little wider, he lifted out a green metal strongbox. It was locked.

"Oh, baby," Mr. Pickens said to a framed photo of F.X. that sat on the chest of drawers; F.X. had his arm around two women who often appeared on game shows as celebrity guests. "I got you now, you little faggot."

There was a wrench and pliers in one of the kitchen drawers, he remembered, but when he tried them out on the strongbox, he got nowhere with them. He needed something bigger, a crowbar or metal rod, something with good leverage.

On his way to the tool shed in the backyard he stumbled on a rake lying in the grass. As he tossed it aside he noticed Mrs. Wedge sitting by her kitchen window. She was eating a bowl of cereal or something and staring out at the dark, moonless night like it was the TV. Keeping an eye on her, he walked into the teeth of the rake again.

The door to the tool shed was ajar. Stepping inside, he reached out with one hand for the string that turned on the naked light bulb. His other hand rested on the aquarium he had bought years ago when he thought he might get interested in fish as a hobby. The string—where was that string? He waved his hand around, collecting a few cobwebs in the musty turpentine air.

After he finally found the light and switched it on, he crouched down to untangle himself from a fishhook that had caught on his trouser cuff. Fishing was another hobby that hadn't worked out. The mail-order company he ordered his pole from sent him a shotgun instead, then tried to make him pay for it. Luckily Mr. Herbert fixed everything up for him, but by that time he didn't feel like fishing anymore. The hook out, he noticed a crowbar lying beside a bag of charcoal briquettes. Picking it up, he smiled. It was good and heavy, solid as could be.

As he turned, crowbar in hand, he noticed a shoe balanced on a bag of lawn fertilizer, the toe pointing toward the ceiling, as if the shoe were defying gravity. Mr. Pickens took a step toward it, mystified, then froze.

F.X. was sprawled out on the damp earth floor of the shed, his foot resting on the fertilizer, his arms covering his head. On his brown chest something white and lustrous gleamed, as beautiful as a pearl. Mr. Pickens gazed at it, entranced, until he realized what it was: a tooth—and everything went black.

J. Peake Jones Memorial looked more like a motel than a hospital, and a small motel at that, not half as big as a Holiday Inn. Mr. Pickens wandered down a dimly lit hall, past several empty rooms, looking for the young man who had driven the ambulance from Sweetgum—Frank was his name. He had a blond goatee and long sideburns, and he seemed to know a lot about what you were supposed to do when you found someone beat up on your property. Mr. Pickens wasn't sure, but when he was riding in the back of the ambulance with F.X., he thought he heard Frank radioing the parish sheriff's office. After they got to the hospital, though, no officer was waiting for them. After F.X. was wheeled away, Mr. Pickens filled out a short form, then was told by a homely pinch-faced woman in a beige pantsuit to go sit in the lobby. He went, assuming that there he would be questioned by the police. But after waiting ten minutes by himself he got too nervous and set off to find Frank.

As he continued his search down the almost deserted halls

his anxiety increased. The longer he waited to talk to the authorities, the more suspicious the whole thing would look. But he had never reported anything to the police before in his life, and he didn't want to do it wrong. If Frank had already requested an officer to come, and Mr. Pickens called and got another, they might get mad at him, and he might be penalized in some legal way. It was so important that everything be on the up and up.

Outside the room where F.X. was being X-rayed Mr. Pickens stopped a young Polynesian-looking girl, a nurse's aide, and asked her if she knew where the ambulance drivers congregated. She didn't. But she had a kind smile and wanted to know if anything was wrong, so Mr. Pickens, who by now felt he just had to talk to someone, told her about his dilemma, asking whether he should call the sheriff's office or not, and if so, were they listed in the book or should he dial 911, the emergency number, even though strictly speaking it was no longer an emergency?

"Uh-uh, man. You no call fuzz," the girl said.

"But something terrible's happened to my brother. He won't tell me anything. I tried to find out in the ambulance, but he wouldn't say a word."

The girl shook her head. "This no good. You listen to Tina. Them filthy pigs, them fuzz. Hit people."

"But . . ." Something inside Mr. Pickens told him this girl was right. He felt a choking sensation. What was he going to say to the police? *Well, officer, I was going out to the tool shed for a crowbar so I could smash open my brother's strongbox.* No, of course that would never work. How about: *Well, officer, I was going out to the tool shed to get some charcoal . . .* A barbecue on a cold November night? Alone? With Mrs. Quaid and the lawyer woman ready to testify against him? Perjury. Jail.

"But listen," Mr. Pickens said to the girl, his heart smothered with anxiety, "you just can't have bad things happen and then not report them, can you?"

"You keep mouth shut. Dukes of Huzza, *they* keep mouth shut."

"Who? What?"

"Uh, oh," she said, seeing the homely woman in the beige suit approach. The woman gave the Polynesian girl a cold look, and the girl hurried away.

Mr. Pickens leaned against the wall and tried to take his pulse, but he could feel nothing beating in his wrist. Maybe he was in a state of shock, he thought. Maybe ever since he had fainted in the tool shed he had been in a state of shock and didn't know what he was doing. So when the police asked him why he didn't report the beating immediately after it happened, he could reply with the absolute truth on his side, "I was in a state of shock."

The door to the X-ray room opened, and a lanky man in a brown uniform walked out. He yawned, stretched his arms, patted the holster on his belt, then reached in his pocket.

"Got a light?" he asked Mr. Pickens as he pulled out a pack of Lucky Strikes.

Mr. Pickens's eyes glazed over. "I didn't . . . you see . . . no, but . . ." His eyebrow began to twitch.

The officer's lined, windburned face remained impassive as he surveyed Mr. Pickens from head to toe. Then he turned, spat into the shiny cuspidor, and walked over to the woman in beige, who gave him a light. They both disappeared, she down the hall, the officer through a pair of swinging doors.

Inside the X-ray room Mr. Pickens found his brother by himself, lying on a table. His face looked worse than it had in the ambulance, even though now all the blood had been washed away. The yellows and purples and reds of the bruises and cuts seemed more garish, and his lips were puffed up like two overripe figs. Mr. Pickens's eyes filled with tears. He didn't know where to look.

"F.X.," he whispered, glancing fearfully at the machine directly overhead. "It's me, Bobby."

F.X.'s eyes were swollen shut, a yellow mucus caked on the lashes. "You asshole," he said, his lips hardly moving. "What'd you call the . . ." He breathed heavily through his mouth. ". . . call the fucking cops for?"

"F.X., I didn't. I swear I didn't. But why not? I mean, this is awful. You ought to see yourself. Can't you tell me what happened? Who did this to you, F.X.? Who? I'd like to break his fucking neck. I swear, I get my hands on him and—"

"You."

"What?"

"I told the cop you did it."

"*Me!*"

"Quiet, the doctor."

"But F.X., *me*? You can't say that."

"Son, please, don't make me talk. Hurts like hell." His hand rose, then fell back to the table. "I had to tell them something, so it was you. Beat me up. Family argument, blah, blah, not pressing charges. Case closed."

"They might arrest—"

"Case closed. Now shut the fuck up. The doctor's coming back and . . . Just remember, you. It was you, son."

The door swung open, and a woman wearing sunglasses strode in with a chart in her hand. Seeing Mr. Pickens, she raised her sunglasses and pointed to the door.

"I'm a relative," Mr. Pickens said.

The doctor kept on pointing to the door. Mr. Pickens backed out of the room. "I'll be out here, doctor, if anything . . ."

When the door swung shut, Mr. Pickens heard F.X. let out

a moan that made Mr. Pickens search out a seat to collapse into. He could not think anymore; all he could do was feel the hurt with a heart as bruised and battered as his brother's face.

CHAPTER

Twenty-four

While Toinette was in the ladies' room Mr. Pickens ordered two more bourbon and diet Dr Peppers; Toinette had got tired of Tab colas. Junior's was jam-packed that night, the jukebox, up as loud as it could go, almost drowned by the farmers and day laborers gabbing three deep at the bar. Seeing Mr. Pickens sitting alone, Mr. Ames, the old man who serviced the vending machines in Tula Springs, sat down in the booth with him. The old man looked something like Khrushchev, and all he ever talked about was his tomatoes, but Mr. Pickens was polite anyway and told him he would love to sit and have a drink with him, but he was on a date. Mr. Ames looked cross-eyed at Mr. Pickens—the old man's idea of a joke—and hoisted himself out of the booth. He had keys, scores of them, hanging from fancy key-rings attached to his belt.

Technically Mr. Pickens wasn't on a date. Toinette had come by the house earlier that evening demanding to see F.X., who had just been released from the hospital. F.X. wasn't allowing anyone to see him, especially Toinette. She and Mr. Pickens had engaged in a short struggle outside F.X.'s room, but it hadn't made any difference that Toinette won, since F.X. had locked the door. Toinette then started whimpering, so Mr. Pickens tried to cheer her up by offering to buy her a drink. She told him to go to hell and hit him on the ear with her hairbrush. After that she felt better and allowed him to take her out. She was dying to know just what had happened to F.X.

At first Toinette was upset when she heard F.X. got beat up. But when Mr. Pickens explained that it was he, Bobby Pickens, who had done the beating up, and that was why F.X. didn't want to see her—he was too ashamed—Toinette started laughing, then grabbed Mr. Pickens by the collar and told him to come straight with her or she'd scratch his eyes out.

"It's the truth, I swear," Mr. Pickens said, holding up his hand. "See, I found out about his plan, the plan to make him a celebrity."

The air seemed to go out of Toinette as she freed his collar and sank back, deflated, in the red plastic booth. For a while she pretended she didn't know what in the world he was talking about, but he had too much evidence against her.

"I was so mad when I heard about this," Mr. Pickens went on. "The first thing hit me was you. I said to myself, 'Bobby, you going to let this girl ruin her life for a damn-fool stunt like this? You going to sit back while that ape gets her thrown in jail?' No, sir. I was boiling, Toinette. You ask Burma. Ask your mama. They saw me boiling in Mrs. LaSteele's house just before I went over and gave it to him."

Toinette said her mother *had* said he went bananas, throwing a chair or something around, but she didn't think it had anything to do with her.

"Well, it did. Better believe it. I was riled."

"But—"

"But what? But F.X. is twice as big as me? Got muscles twice as hard? So what. When a person gets riled, doesn't matter how he looks. Haven't you ever heard stories about mothers lifting up trucks and boulders and things so they can yank their little babies out? Well, sir, that's exactly what happened to me."

Toinette's green eyes got darker, widened. But doubt still sketched little bird's feet on her forehead.

"Besides," he said, worried that he wasn't coming across, "I used to do a little boxing at St. Jude. Nothing fancy, but—"

"Bobby, you?"

This was not a total lie. Mr. Pickens had indeed been forced to box in phys. ed. one day, or rather, to put on gloves. The class bell rang, though, before it was his turn to spar.

"Sure. I was a medium." He coughed. "Medium weight."

"But how . . . You seem . . . I mean . . ."

"Hey, Toin. So I don't go around bragging." He shrugged and looked over nonchalantly at the bar. His eyebrows went up like F.X.'s sometimes did. "So, like, what can I say? People aren't always what they seem. You get a little older and you'll find out I'm right."

Toinette sat there a moment, trying to digest this. "Now, look here," she said, flaring up suddenly, "who asked *you* to be the big hero? I could kill Burma. She should've kept her trap shut. And you—you go butting in where you don't belong. Why, hell, Bobby, I was on the verge of becoming famous."

Mr. Pickens's eyebrows went up again. He sighed in a worldly way, still staring at the bar. "Famous, huh? Toin, if you were serious about being famous, you never would have blabbed to Burma. But you were scared, weren't you? You knew well as anyone what would happen to you. A laughing-stock, at the very least."

"You think you're so smart."

He smiled vaguely, looking at her with half-closed eyes.

"Oh," she exclaimed with a stamp of her foot.

Grabbing her purse, she stood up and headed for the ladies' room, leaving Mr. Pickens alone and not at all displeased with his performance. Of course, as a rule he hated telling lies. But surely this was a different case; God couldn't hold this against him. He wanted to help F.X., and the only way he could do so was to lie and say he had beaten him up. Besides, by sticking with this story and promising not to go to the parish police with the real story, Mr. Pickens had got Toinette's watch back (it was not in the strongbox; it was tucked inside a pair of F.X.'s sweat socks), which meant that after tossing it into Tula Creek (which he promptly did) he had nothing more to worry about.

Only F.X. and Mr. Pickens knew the real story. The truth was, F.X. had hooked up with an old buddy from Angola who was supplying him with cocaine. The plan was to sell just enough to a few professors at St. Jude—it wasn't big time; he wasn't going to be greedy—to be able to afford the services of a press agent F.X. knew in Los Angeles, a good friend of Elizabeth, his former wife's. The agent worked with top stars, big names, and promised to handle F.X. if he could come up with a substantial down payment in coke. With a pro like this stirring up the publicity that would come from the Tula Springs rape, F.X. knew he couldn't miss. The only trouble was, some gentlemen in New Orleans were not too pleased that F.X. was underpricing them at St. Jude. So they paid him a visit to make sure he understood that it wasn't such a good idea to sell dope in Louisiana.

When F.X. confessed all this, saying he'd rather die than end up back in Angola, Mr. Pickens felt a little less sorry for him. He wanted to say, *I hope this taught you a good lesson*, but he didn't. Maybe when F.X. felt well enough to get out of bed, he'd say it.

When he saw Toinette coming out of the ladies' room, Mr.

Pickens stood up. Her feet splayed out a little when she walked, which made his heart beat faster.

"Hi," he said.

They both sat down. Somewhat sullenly Toinette began to sip her drink, tapping one finger in time to the jukebox. In the corner near the pool table Mr. Ames looked up from the electronic Space Invaders game he was playing. He gaped at them, then gaped at a blue light in the ceiling.

Mr. Pickens looked up from his drink and found Toinette staring at him. They both quickly looked away.

"I just can't figure out why you went along with him," he said, scratching the allergy itch on his arm. "You should've just laughed in his face."

"It's this town," she snapped. "I hate it. There's nothing to do 'cept get drunk. And everyone's a creep."

"Then why don't you move somewhere else, like Baton Rouge?"

"I'm not a big-city person. Besides, I finally found someone who isn't a creep, who isn't dull as a toad." She looked hard at him. "I'm in love, mister."

He picked at the red skin of an oily peanut. "So am I," he said, immediately regretting it. Now was not the time to say it. What was wrong with him?

"I know," she said, popping a peanut into her mouth. "Mama told me."

"Told you?"

"I said to her, 'Mama, what you getting so worked up about? So Emmet and Bobby's in love. They got stuff like that on TV all the time.'"

"We were praying," he said, bringing his hand down on the Formica table. "How many times I got to tell everybody, we were praying!"

"Burma believes you." She smiled disingenuously. "Burma

believes anything you say. I swear, you got that girl wrapped around your little finger. Emmet's so jealous. They had a big fight about you, you know."

Mr. Pickens sighed.

"I was there, I heard them." Toinette's eyes sparkled. "There was this commercial with George Washington come on, and for no reason at all Burma says, 'Bobby doesn't like the way George Washington looks,' and Emmet says, 'Who the hell cares what George Washington looks like?' and the next thing you know, they're both getting all worked up— Emmet's shy, so it takes him a longer time to get worked up. I never seen him like that. His face was all red, and he starts accusing and stuff, and Burma"—Toinette helped herself to a few more peanuts—"Burma, she says, 'There's nothing dirty between me and Bobby Pickens. He's like a brother. And besides, he's turning into a preacher.' So I say, 'Right, girl, *some* preacher. He goes around stealing watches and Lord knows what else and . . .' Hey, that reminds me, I want that watch back. F.X. doesn't need it no more. I want it back."

"Listen, you never gave me a chance to explain. I didn't steal your watch, Toinette. Honest."

"Then what was it doing in your dresser drawer? That's just where F.X. found it, Reverend."

"Remember when you set it down on the candy counter? I thought it'd be a good joke if I—"

"Ha, ha, very funny." A wisp of red hair was caught in the clasp of her necklace. She became preoccupied trying to untangle it.

"Here," he said, reaching out to help her.

"So where is it?" she said, slapping away his hand. "That watch cost me. It took practically all my savings."

"Be reasonable," he said, wondering now if it had been such a good idea to throw the watch in the river.

The hair came loose. She pushed her half-filled glass of bourbon and diet Dr Pepper away. "Go get me a glass of rosé wine, Bobby. And make sure Junior don't put any water in it."

Junior poured the wine from a gallon jug he kept under the bar. When Mr. Pickens handed him three quarters, plus a dime tip, Junior winked at him. "That your lady?" he asked, nodding toward Toinette.

Mr. Pickens smiled uncertainly.

"She's a honey," Junior said, grabbing a handful of beer mugs. A red-faced man at the bar looked over his shoulder to see who Junior was talking about.

Flushed with pride, Mr. Pickens made his way through the noisy crowd, cradling the wine in both hands so that not a drop would be spilled.

CHAPTER

Twenty-five

As they walked slowly down the path trying to avoid the roots and stones that could trip them up, the dinette table got tangled in a patch of cow-itch vine. Donna Lee put down her end of the table and yanked on the vine, which skirted a large magnolia. Breathing hard, Burma clung to the back end of the table and looked distrustfully at the woods around them. In the pale autumn light the waxy magnolia leaves gleamed with a coffee-table shine, while on either side of the overgrown footpath unseen birds rooting through fallen river-birch leaves sounded big as ostriches. A squirrel paused

to scold the intruders, then continued its search for nuts
among the silvery branches of a bitter pecan.

With a final yank the table came loose, and the women
continued along the path. They were headed for the Josie
Wayne Bickell Recreation Center on the banks of Tula
Creek. Fifteen years ago, when blacks could no longer be
excluded from Josie Wayne, Tula Springs discovered it had
no more funds for the center's upkeep. Aside from the occasional teenagers looking for an out-of-the-way place to neck,
Josie Wayne had had no visitors until the previous week,
when Donna Lee, armed with a mop, a broom, and a gallon
of ammonia, came to take charge. Burma had finally broken
down and explained why she was prowling through the house
on Sweetgum, and as Donna Lee should have guessed, Pickens
was in the thick of it with a stolen watch and his crazy, schem-
ing brother. After listening to Burma's story Donna Lee decided right then and there that a firm hand had to be taken,
or this girl, whom she had grown rather fond of, would be
lost for good.

First of all, Burma should not be living at home. Donna
Lee considered it unhealthy for a thirty-seven-year-old to be
so close to her mother. Furthermore, Donna Lee did not like
the idea of a boyfriend living under the same roof with the
mother and daughter; it was not right. Was it any wonder
Burma was so confused, living in that pink hothouse? A good
healthy dose of nature—fresh air, trees, a river—would be
just the thing to get her muddled head straightened out.

Burma, though, was making things difficult. The other
day, when she had come out to look at the place with Donna
Lee, Burma had started crying. She said a basketball court
wasn't her idea of a living room. (It wasn't actually a real,
full-size basketball court—just a few lines painted on the
cement floor.) And she thought the urinal in the men's room

(she had never seen a urinal before) was downright porno-graphic. Donna Lee told her to stop her foolishness. There were millions of people all over the world who would give their right arm to live in a place as nice as Josie Wayne. Just look at those big sinks over by the Coke machine. What apartment, what house in all of Tula Springs had sinks as big as those? And this was rent free! Burma would be able to save her salary for the wedding like she wanted to. After they gave the place another good scrubbing and got rid of that little sumac that had poked through the floor near the foul line, all Burma would need were a few sticks of furniture to make everything look nice and homey.

If anything, though, the few sticks of furniture they lugged through the woods made Josie Wayne look even more for-lorn. Donna Lee, however, was determined not to admit this as they set the dinette table down beside a decrepit leather vaulting horse. She studied the horse for a moment, wonder-ing how it could be domesticated. It was too heavy for them to throw away. With a quilt over it, though, it might make a nice valet. Donna Lee sighed and plugged in the brass stand-ing lamp she had borrowed from her father's too-cluttered den.

"See, I *was* able to get the electricity turned on," she said with unconvincing cheer. It had taken half the morning to do it. Donna Lee had had to pretend she was a town official, since only the town could be billed for this electricity. Luck-ily she had a friend in City Hall who gave her a billing authori-zation number that Louisiana Power and Light accepted.

Burma just stood there next to the battered Coke ma-chine, frowning at the wing chair Donna Lee had provided from her own apartment, the Audubon print of a rain crow above the chair, the coffee table from Mrs. LaSteele's house (Donna Lee had convinced her that she was entitled to it since she had been paying her mother's utility bills), the dinette set (bought with an employee's discount at Sonny Boy), and finally the swinging slatted doors to the men's and ladies' rooms, on which Donna Lee had hung maps of Louisiana's waterways.

"What's wrong?" Donna Lee demanded. "Don't you like it?"

Burma hitched up her purple slacks. "I just don't feel right not paying any rent. What if someone catches me here?"

"Look, hon, I told you, you're doing the town a favor. You'll keep the place in shape. They ought to pay *you* for staying here."

"It smells funny."

"A little air and . . ." Donna Lee said, shoving on a window that wouldn't open.

"And it's so damp. Mama would die if she saw me out here. Just wait till she gets back from Cairo. She'll murder me." She went over to the horse and put her finger into a rip in its side. "I still don't see why I can't have Emmet come stay with me."

"Someone has to look after your mother's house."

"That's not the real reason."

Donna Lee was red-faced from trying to open the window. She gave up and moved to another.

"You don't like Emmet, do you?" Burma said.

"I have no opinion one way or another. Ah, look, here it comes."

"I'm freezing."

The window creaked up slowly. Donna Lee stuck her head outside. "Burma, come over here and breathe. It's great. Look, there's a robin."

Burma stayed where she was. "What Miss Quaid said that night about Bobby and Emmet, it ain't true. They're just good friends, that's all."

Donna Lee pulled in her head. "I know. That has nothing to do with it."

"Then why can't Emmet come on out here?"

"Look, how many times do I have to explain? You're here to spend time alone, getting to know yourself, trying to find out who the real you is, what Burma LaSteele really wants out of life."

"I already know what I want. I want to get married, dammit."

Donna Lee picked up a push broom and began to sweep away some sawdust. "Frankly, Burma, I don't think you're ready for marriage yet."

"Not ready? All I got to do is buy the stamps for the envelopes. Bobby's done finished the invitations and—"

"Hush. Now just listen to yourself. There it is again: Bobby Pickens. Why can't you have a discussion without throwing in his name?"

"I don't throw in his name. Besides, I'm just proud of him, that's all. No one seems to realize how much courage that boy has. F.X. is twice as big, and yet he—"

"Please, spare me. I've heard it all before. Now, look, instead of just standing there making that rip bigger, why don't you go get the Ajax and start scrubbing out the sinks. I want to cook you a nice meal tonight."

They had brought along a Coleman stove, which was sitting on the counter next to a wok, a gift from Donna Lee. She was going to teach Burma how to prepare nourishing vegetarian meals. Afterward she planned to restyle Burma's hair, getting rid of those pageboy bangs. Then she was going to accidentally lose Burma's elaborate makeup kit, so she could show her how it was possible to look nice with only a few essentials.

The women worked silently for a quarter of an hour, each

absorbed in her own thoughts. When Donna Lee went outside to shake the hooked rug, she got a head start on the cocktail hour by sipping from the Thermos of martinis she had prepared at home. Burma was getting on her nerves. She just didn't seem to appreciate anything. After all the work Donna Lee had done for her in the past few days, was there one thank you? Hardly. Burma bitched and groused the whole time as if she were having her teeth pulled, and Donna Lee did not like to think of herself as a dentist.

After bringing the rug back inside Donna Lee went to a sink and began washing alfalfa sprouts. She was feeling very relaxed now as she chewed her Clorets thoughtfully.

"This sink won't get clean," Burma said, throwing down her soap pad. She had been scrubbing mildew off the adjacent sink. "I hate this place. I'm not going to stay here one more minute."

"Hon," Donna Lee said, setting the colander of sprouts aside, "come on."

"What?"

Donna Lee took her by the arm in a formal way, like a gentleman escorting a lady in evening clothes, and walked outside with her past the slide and jungle gym to the riverbank. Floating on the teak-dark waters were rosy bouquets of light reflected from clouds flushed with the setting sun. Across the river Spanish moss stirred in the branches of a half-dead water oak like a gossamer negligee. Burma buttoned up her fluffy sweater against the cold.

"Look," Donna Lee said, "just look. This is your home now—not that old hall back there, but this. Could anyone ask for anything more beautiful? How lucky you are, Burma! How I envy you."

Burma waved away a cloud of gnats. "Why don't you take Josie Wayne, then, and I'll take your apartment."

Donna Lee felt a twinge of annoyance. "Hon, try to understand: There's so much poison you *must* get out of your system. Believe me, after a few days out here you won't recognize yourself. You'll be a new person."

"What's wrong with the old me?"

"Nothing—except that you're thoroughly miserable, confused, and overweight." Donna Lee didn't mean to be quite so harsh. She blushed, turning away to stare at the water oak; then, remorseful, she put her arm around Burma, whose eyes were filled with tears.

"Dear, you mustn't listen to what I say."

"You're right, though," Burma said. "I feel like you can see right through me, Donna Lee. It's sort of scary."

"I'm sorry—I don't mean to come on so strong. It's just that I think you have so much potential. You're really a very attractive woman, Burma—I wish my complexion were as nice as yours—but I don't think you think of yourself as being attractive. That's not right. You begin to let other people run your life, and before you know it, you have no idea what *you* want."

Burma was shivering in her bright-green sweater. "I *am* all mixed up, Donna Lee. I mean, Emmet's been so nice to me; he's the only man I've met that makes me feel pretty. I know he doesn't have the good qualities Bobby has, the brains and the morals and stuff. But Bobby and me, really, we don't have the right chemicals between us. I feel so pure with him, like he was my brother, you know. And besides, what does he care about me? He's in love with Toinette."

"No one says you *have* to get married."

"What's that?"

"I said, no one says—"

"No," she said, pointing up in the air. "That big ugly bird. Oh, Lord, look."

Soaring in a thermal draft, a turkey vulture suddenly swooped low over a tupelo gum black with other, roosting vultures.

"Honey, it's only crows," Donna Lee lied, and then she tried to distract her by pretending to see a deer on a nearby sandpit. But Burma kept her eyes fixed on the bare-limbed tupelo gum, whose knees, poking out of the dark water, looked sleek as snake heads.

"Come on, Burma. Let's go back and have a drink. It'll warm you up."

Twenty-six

Mr. Pickens had moved into the den, giving F.X. his bedroom while he recovered. The first operation on F.X.'s nose had been a rough, utilitarian job of reopening the passages in the smashed cartilage so that he could breathe decently. F.X. was supposed to go to a specialist in Baton Rouge in a few days to get the nose shaped like it used to look.

"So the man from the glass company said he'd give us a discount on colored glass, like for a green pane where the cardboard is," Mr. Pickens was saying to F.X., who was propped up in bed with a TV tray in front of him. Mr. Pickens had brought him a catfish dinner from Iota's.

"I let him put in the green pane," Mr. Pickens went on, "then the glass man says since you got a green pane, it might look nice to have the window all different colors. Then Mrs.

Wedge comes over and asks the glass man if he'd come next door and hold the ladder for her while she pulls some ivy off her roof gutter. I ask her if she wouldn't mind waiting until the glass man was through with me, seeing as how I'm paying him and everything, and she gets on her high horse and says, 'Thank you, Mr. Pickens. Here I am half dead with grief, and you got to keep the glass man all to yourself.' I ask her what's the matter, and she says that Motor—that's the orange cat—Motor ate one of her little kittens. They were just born yesterday, and Mrs. Wedge wants to know if we want one."

F.X. picked up the catfish with his hand and bit into it.

"You want a kitten, F.X.?"

"Where you going? I smell my Pierre Cardin."

Mr. Pickens had already explained to F.X. he was just going out to a movie at the mall. He did not mention, though, that Toinette was his date. "The Twin Cinemas. There's this werewolf movie I've been meaning to see."

A little furtively Mr. Pickens raised the window shade. Near the ditch out back the mimosas, bare except for a few pods, looked brittle as coral in the purple dusk. As if a wave were washing over them, the tall grasses by the tool shed bent to a stiff breeze that exposed their silvery undersides. Mr. Pickens felt his stomach tighten; he could not look at the shed without feeling a dull ache.

"Shut that shade." When F.X. talked now, his clogged nose made him sound like Marlon Brando.

"It's so dark," Mr. Pickens said, pulling down the shade. "Don't you want a light on?"

"I smell Pierre Cardin."

Mr. Pickens bumped into the chest of drawers as he headed for the door. He had indeed borrowed some of F.X.'s cologne.

"I told you, I'm fixing to go to the movies."

He leaned over and wiped a mud spot off his new boots,

which made him a couple of inches taller. Mr. Pickens had bought them at the mall that afternoon on impulse, after having bought three pairs of designer jeans. The jeans were so tight they gave him a stomachache, and he had to roll them under because they didn't have a size for legs as short as his.

"You need Pierre Cardin for a werewolf movie? That shit's expensive."

"Look, F.X., I need to get out. All day long I'm cooped up in that office. Then I come home, and all we do is sit and watch the TV. You never want to *do* anything."

The previous week, after having been turned down for a position on the Tula Springs *Herald* (Mrs. Jenks told him he dangled too many things—participles and stuff), Mr. Pickens had accepted the job Burma had urged him to try out for. Mr. Herbert and Donna Lee needed someone to help out in the law office while their receptionist had her baby. If Mr. Pickens hadn't been desperate for money—his unemployment compensation had run out, and the only other job he was offered was that of bookkeeper/nightwatchman at the Tula Springs Hatcheries, and he just hated live chickens—he never would have accepted the job. He was still mad at Donna Lee for sending him a threatening letter about the dent in her Volvo. Now that she was his boss, he thought this would be the end of that stupid business. But just today she had brought up the dent again and asked him if it wouldn't be fair for her to dock him a few dollars each week until the dent was paid for. He said no, it would not be fair, and was amazed how this incident almost ruined his daydreams about the upcoming date with Toinette.

After offering to run over to Dr. Henry's to buy F.X. a Slush Puppie to drink and getting a sullen shrug as a reply, Mr. Pickens went back into the den. He was getting tired of trying to cheer up his brother all the time. It was like coming home to a great big albatross every night, an albatross that didn't give a damn about anyone's problems but its own. Mr. Pickens stood in front of the full-length mirror to see how the jeans made him look. He turned from side to side, craning his neck over his shoulder for a back view, then picked up one of F.X.'s dumbbells.

He was lifting the dumbbell to his chest for the fifth time— a new record—when the door chimes rang.

It was Toinette. He had *told* her he would drive by and pick her up at her house. What the hell was going on?

"Relax," she said as they stood out on the porch. "I just figured Mama would get all worked up if she seen you. I'm not allowed to date degenerates, you know." She tweaked his cheek and strode into the house.

"Oh, nice, you got a church window," Toinette said, looking at the newly installed stained glass. She pulled a fuzzy wool poncho over her head, revealing, as the static electricity crackled, a skimpy evening dress that shimmered like the bluish scales on a dragonfly.

"Let's get going," Mr. Pickens said softly, urgently, while holding open the front door.

Toinette flounced onto the love seat. "Boy, let me catch my breath."

"Come on." He gestured fiercely, but it was too late.

"What is *she* doing here?" F.X. stood in the entrance hall wearing the brown pajamas Mr. Pickens had bought him. "I thought I told you I didn't want her setting foot in this house anymore."

Toinette's hand went to her mouth; her eyes widened. It was the first time she had seen F.X. since he got beat up. "My God, your face, your poor face. Bobby, what did you do to him? How could you?" She hurried across the room to F.X., but he pushed her away.

"Bobby?" he said. "What did *he* do?"

"F.X., you poor baby." She wiped away a tear.

"Get out of here," F.X. said, turning on her suddenly. He grabbed her roughly by the shoulder and shoved her out the front door, slamming it behind her.

"Now suppose we have a little talk, Bobby."

Mr. Pickens retreated toward the love seat. "Take it easy, F.X. I can explain."

"You told her you beat me up?" F.X. said, taking another step forward. "You?"

"But that's what you told me to say, isn't it?"

"To the cops, asshole. Just in case they questioned you. I told you we were through with Toinette."

"I *had* to tell her something. And I was afraid if I told her the truth, it might leak out to Burma and all, and you'd end up back in jail. I couldn't stand it if you ended up in Angola again, honest. I was just trying to help."

"What were you talking to her for? I told you we were through with her. She doesn't need any explanations, nothing. What is she, anyway? Just a goddamn slut with a big mouth. Sluts aren't entitled to explanations."

"Now, look here, F.X. Don't you go calling her—"

F.X. reached out and grabbed Mr. Pickens by the neck. His grip was so strong it made Mr. Pickens's eyes bulge. "You threatening me, son?"

Mr. Pickens gasped and coughed hoarsely. The grip relaxed, but when Mr. Pickens tried to struggle free, he felt F.X.'s other hand clamp down painfully on his bicep. F.X. shoved him up against the mantel.

"You made a fool out of me, didn't you? Everyone in town thinks you beat me up." He stuck his face right next to Mr. Pickens's. "Couldn't keep your frigging mouth shut, could you, boy? Not even for your own brother. Wasn't bad enough

I lost my looks, but now you got to ruin my reputation too, huh? Oh, son, that is evil, plain evil."

"F.X., please, you're hurting me."

F.X. grimaced, as if he were the one in pain, and squeezed Mr. Pickens's arm so tight that Mr. Pickens yelped.

"Stop! Help!" Mr. Pickens cried, his face damp with sweat. He tried to pry loose the hand that still held his inflamed neck.

The umbrella stand clattered over as the front door was flung open. "My poncho," Toinette said angrily, pointing at the wrap on the love seat. "I came to get my— Bobby, get your dirty hands off him!"

She ran across the living room and began to pummel Mr. Pickens. "Leave him alone!" she screamed, kicking off a mauve high heel. While she reached down to pick it up Mr. Pickens retreated behind the love seat. "You touch him and I'll kill you," she said through clenched teeth, brandishing the heel.

F.X. groaned. "You stupid bitch."

She looked stricken. "Oh, F.X., please, give me a chance. Are you all right, baby? He didn't hurt you? Please let me talk. Don't you know how sorry I am? I could die when I think what I did. I don't blame you for being mad at me. I should've kept my mouth shut. I shouldn't have said a word to Burma about our secret, I know. But now that's all past. We can start over again. I'll do anything you want, anything. F.X., I love you."

"Get out." He jerked his arm away. She had clasped it and now tried to hold on to it again. But he yanked hard, too hard, and his arm, coming free, accidentally smacked her on the side of the head. She tumbled to the floor, landing on her rear end.

Mr. Pickens hurried to her side. "You satisfied?" he said bitterly, looking up at F.X.

Toinette sat there with a dazed look on her face while Mr. Pickens stuffed her foot into the high heel. Then he helped her stand up.

At the door she paused a moment, clutching the poncho to her bosom. "I feel sorry for you, F.X.," she said in a weak, distant voice. "I really do. 'Cause there's nothing worse than a person can't love. Bobby, he's twice the man you are, F.X. You understand?"

Mr. Pickens hung his head. F.X. kept his bruised face averted.

"Hey, Bobby," she said as he headed toward the den, "where you going? We got plans tonight, boy. We're fixing to have ourselves some fun. Come on. We'll take my car."

CHAPTER

Twenty-seven

Mr. Pickens stood at the urinal in Josie Wayne's men's room. He had been drinking a lot that evening and needed to go bad, but he was too stiff. He and Toinette hadn't gone to the were-wolf movie. Instead they had brought four six-packs to the sand beach near Junior's, where he felt like a fraud the whole time they made out. He wanted to tell her the truth—that he hadn't beat up F.X.—but he was afraid if he did, she wouldn't let him kiss her anymore. This was the moment he had dreamed of for so long, except that in his dreams there wasn't clammy wet sand plastered all over her back and arms and he wasn't freezing to death. He pleaded with her to go back to the car with him—he had a wild hope he might persuade her to check into the Pontchartrain Courts with him in Ozone—but she insisted on staying out on the beach. They kissed, but he wasn't allowed to touch her breasts or anything below her waist. Then all of a sudden she broke away from his embrace and went to the river and threw up. It was the beer, she said. She threw up again a few minutes later and started crying, which is how they ended up at Josie Wayne. She made him drive her out there so she could make up with Burma, whom she had stopped speaking to because of her big mouth.

When Mr. Pickens came out of the men's room, Burma told him Toinette had gone on home. She said Toinette said to tell him she was too depressed to pretend like she was having a good time and she was sorry for running out like this. Mr. Pickens said he understood, then sat down in front of the TV set, furious.

"Bobby, you think you ought to have that?" Burma asked as he popped open the last can of beer. The others had been consumed while Burma and Toinette had taken a walk, leaving Mr. Pickens with nothing to do but watch TV. He tilted back his head and chugalugged the whole can.

Burma sighed. Her face looked different without a lot of makeup on. She looked older, somehow. And she had a new hairstyle that Mr. Pickens couldn't decide whether he liked or not. There were no bangs, so her face looked bigger. All in all she made him vaguely uncomfortable. People shouldn't try to change their looks overnight. Life had enough surprises as it was.

"Do we have to have this on?" she asked, switching off the TV. "It's all I do, watch TV. There's nothing else to do out here." She sat down in the wing chair. "By the way, don't tell

Donna Lee I got this TV, okay? I'm supposed to be looking at birds and trees and stuff. And she give me this book to read about this Swedish lady who raises coffee in Africa, but nothing happens to her, she talks too much about the scenery, you know, so I don't think I'll be able to finish it. Bobby?"

"Huh?"

Burma crossed her legs and smoothed out her gray skirt. He wasn't used to seeing her in such subdued colors; she also had on a silky ivory blouse with a smudge on it, and a charcoal jacket. "What do you think of her—Donna Lee? She must be pretty smart if she made it all the way through law school, right? But there's something so sad about her. I mean, you ought to see her apartment. It really made me depressed just to look at it—no nice furniture, no pictures, nothing. I told her she ought to come by Sonny Boy at lunch hour someday, and I'd help her pick out a few throw rugs, maybe some curtains . . . oh, and some pillows too. A few pillows for accent can really liven up a place. And Bobby, the way she eats—weeds and things I wouldn't feed to a dog, uh uh." Burma shook her head vigorously. "Anyway, the minute I laid eyes on her, something deep down inside me said, 'That girl needs you, Burma. You be her friend.' Believe me, though, it isn't easy. She can be a little bossy. It's like she's simmering all the time, waiting to blow up at you. So I go along with her just to keep the peace." Burma reached for a can on the coffee table and sprayed a strange-looking bug that wandered over a *Ms.* magazine. "But don't get me wrong, Bobby. I do admire her a whole lot. And I really think I'll be able to help her. All she needs is a good man—that ought to do the trick. She could be so good-looking if she wanted—she slouches, you know, and she doesn't smile enough. It's important for a girl to smile and look pleasant at all times. Something that simple and basic Donna Lee never heard of. But I haven't got the nerve to tell her yet. I'm biding my time. . . . Carl Robert Pickens, what are you doing? My Lord, you put that shirt back on."

Mr. Pickens tossed the cowboy shirt away; it landed on the sumac near the foul line. He leaned over and tugged at his boots.

Burma stood up, her hands on her hips.

"I'm tired," Mr. Pickens said as he slipped off the designer jeans, which left a red band around his belly.

"I'll drive you home, then. Now, stop your nonsense."

"Tired of mendacity," Mr. Pickens said, grabbing the chair arm for balance. He stood before her in his new orange bikini briefs and his matching orange undershirt. His belly button was plainly visible; the underwear was two sizes too small.

"Why pretend?" Mr. Pickens said, pulling the T-shirt over his head. His white hairless chest swelled out into a sizable belly, from which Burma averted her eyes. "You want me," he went on. "You've always wanted me. So here. Take me." He stretched out his arms.

"Mr. Pickens," Burma said, turning away. "Please, get dressed. You're drunk."

"This is your chance, Burma. Why blow it? You're getting old—there's gray in your hair, gray in mine. We're going to die, all of us, we're going to die miserable, unloved. I can't stand it anymore. At least one of us can be happy. You, Burma. You be happy. You deserve it more than any of us. You're good, Burma. You're a good, good woman. I can see your heart. It's pure and unselfish and good." Tears ran down his cheeks and his nose began to run. "Take it. Grab life before it passes you by." He stepped out of the briefs, and she beheld him stark naked, except for his left sock, the one with the hole in it, which he had forgotten to take off.

Burma snatched the shirt off the sumac and with lips pursed began the arduous task of dressing him. "Here," she said, cramming his arm into the sleeve. It was like dressing a five-hundred-pound baby. The arms dangled like deadweights, then jerked spasmodically in the wrong direction. She shoved him into the chair to get the pants back on.

"Disgusting," she murmured as he passed out.

CHAPTER

Twenty-eight

"Order late right away," Mr. Herbert mumbled as he passed by Mr. Pickens's desk on his way to the coffee machine.

"Yes, sir," Mr. Pickens replied. A few moments later it occurred to him that Mr. Herbert's request made no sense. Order late right away? Maybe it was "tape," order tape right away. As Mr. Herbert returned down the green corridor past the reception desk Mr. Pickens asked him what he had said. Was it tape—and if so, what kind of tape, Scotch, packing, TRL Dictaphone?

"I think someone in this office needs an appointment with the ear doctor," Mr. Herbert said in answer to Mr. Pickens's question. Then the silver-haired lawyer went into his office and began watering his cactuses.

Mr. Pickens sat there staring at the depositions Donna Lee wanted photocopied right away. If he leaned forward too far, much less stood up, he was sure he would throw up. The pain in his forehead was excruciating; only by holding his head perfectly still at precisely the right angle was he able to survive. He could not remember how he had got home from Burma's the night before. Try as he might, the last thing he could recall was Kate Jackson diving over a car hood on TV. The next thing he knew he was waking up on the sofa in his own den, fully dressed.

All morning Mr. Pickens did his best to appear busy while just sitting at his desk, answering an occasional phone call. Around noon Donna Lee sailed into Mr. Herbert's office with a folder in her hand. The door shut. Intrigued by the severe look on her face and the fact that she had shut the door behind her, Mr. Pickens, his hangover not quite so bad, got up and wandered over to the door with the depositions he still hadn't copied. He could not hear too well, even with his ear pressed against the door. Donna Lee was saying something about a shower, a shocking, horrible shower.

The outer door to the offices gave a ping, warning the receptionist that someone had come inside. Mr. Pickens hurried to his desk, wondering who in the world could be operating an obscene shower, whatever that was. Miss Mina? Lord, he hoped not. For months he hadn't paid her a visit. But then, after F.X. got beat up, it was strange . . . he had seen her twice last week. She could testify against him, even though he had never taken a shower there. Had he? He would lose his job and . . . He knew he should stop seeing her. It was a disgrace.

"Earth to Mr. Pickens, earth to Mr. Pickens, come in, Mr. Pickens," Mr. Keely said, holding out his hand. Mr. Pickens took it and smiled politely.

"Say," Mr. Keely said, scratching his gray crewcut, "we've all been wondering if you're ever coming back to Bible class. Mayor Binwanger has joined us now. And last time Mr. Randy brought along his brother-in-law, Sal something. You'd like Sal, I'm sure. A very interesting young man, shy, but smart, smart as a whip." Mr. Keely seemed distracted for a moment. His eyes wandered over the baby calendar tacked up behind the desk. "Yes, indeed. Say, that's a nice ring." He leaned over for a closer look at Mr. Pickens's St. Jude class ring. "Ummm. By the way, is Ann in?"

"Ann?"

"I mean Donna Lee." He coughed into his fist.

While Mr. Pickens buzzed Mr. Herbert's office Mr. Keely hummed and jiggled the keys in his pocket. Eddie May, the legal secretary, stuck her gray head out the door of her office and waved to Mr. Keely, who didn't notice her. She made a face and went back to her IBM.

"Sugar," Mr. Keely said as Donna Lee came out of Mr. Herbert's office.

"Oh, hi, Dad."

Mr. Keely pecked her on the forehead, then plucked a thread out of her silky blond hair. He cleared his throat. "Your mother was wondering if you could pick Moab up after work today. She's going to help serve tonight at the bridge party."

Donna Lee just looked at him.

"I've got a Kiwanis meeting," he said with a guilty smile. "Be glad to otherwise."

"Oh, all right. Where does she live?"

"Raid Avenue. Two Raid."

"I never heard of Raid."

"It's over by the vet clinic," Mr. Pickens said.

Donna Lee turned to him. "Haven't you run off those depositions yet?" Then to her father: "Is that all? I mean, you could have phoned, you know."

Mr. Keely coughed into his fist. "Yes, well, little stroll, good for the ticker, they say. Hmmm." He shambled over to the door.

"When you get through with the copying," Donna Lee said to Mr. Pickens, "come into my office. I want to talk to you.

Dad," she called out as he was going out the door, "good-bye. Thanks."

Mr. Pickens sat down on the Lady chapel pew. He had just returned from the men's room, where he had discovered he was missing a contact lens. It was that, not the hangover, that was making everything seem so bleary today.

Donna Lee regarded him steadily for a moment. "I hear you're quite a boxer."

He went red in the face. "That was some time ago."

Standing over him, Donna Lee suddenly jabbed out with her fist at his belly. With a spastic jerk his hands flew up to his face. She hadn't touched him.

Going to her desk, she opened a drawer and handed him an envelope.

"You want this copied?" he asked, glancing apprehensively at her. She was really nuts.

"Look inside. You and I will be taking a little trip to Ozone in January. The courthouse."

The damn car dent again. Mr. Pickens looked glumly at the unopened envelope.

"Miss Keely, if you hate me so much, why did you let Mr. Herbert hire me in the first place?"

"I don't hate you, Mr. Pickens. Mr. Herbert's the one who hates you." She jotted down something on a note pad. "In fact, I told him I'd quit if he didn't hire you. He wanted to hire Eddie May's niece. As far as the summons goes, there's nothing personal about it. It's simply a matter of justice. You do believe in justice, don't you, Bobby?" She went back to her writing.

Mr. Pickens sat there, mulling this over.

Donna Lee looked up, sighed. "I'm sorry, Bobby. I didn't mean to sound rude. But you *did* ask." She bit the end of her fountain pen. "If you must know, I got you hired here because Burma LaSteele asked me to. She was very concerned about you. She wouldn't give me any peace until I agreed to take you on. I happen to think a great deal of Burma. In fact, I wanted her to have the job. I thought I might train her to become a legal secretary. But she insisted you needed it more than she did."

"If I'd have known, I'd—"

"You'd have what? Given her the job instead? I doubt it. I doubt you've ever given that woman a second thought."

Mr. Pickens shrugged. He fiddled with the buttons on the Dictaphone machine sitting beside him on the pew. "She's nice."

"Nice," she repeated, shaking her head. "Oh, you men, you blind, foolish men. Tits and ass, huh? That's all you need to make you happy. But take a woman like Burma, someone who's got so much to offer and—"

". . . *you men, you blind, foolish men. Tits and ass, huh? That's all . . .*"

"Turn that off," Donna Lee said sharply, rising out of her chair.

Mr. Pickens fumbled with the buttons, the dial. "Sorry, I didn't realize . . . thought it was . . ."

"Hand that to me."

Red-faced, she took the machine from him and stashed it in her desk drawer.

"A word of advice," she said as he stood by the door. "If I were you, Bobby, I'd start noticing things around me. I'd stop going around with my head in the clouds."

This made Mr. Pickens very uneasy. Was she trying to warn him about Miss Mina's shower? Was there going to be a raid?

Late in the afternoon, just as he was getting ready to go home, the phone rang. All day he had been trying to reach

Toinette at St. Jude to find out how she was feeling. He needed to talk to her bad. But the same girl kept on answering the hall phone in her dorm, a girl who had a mousy voice and didn't seem too good at remembering messages.

Mr. Pickens was filled with hope when he said, "Good morning, Mr. Herbert's office. May I help you?"

"Bobby?"

"Oh, it's you." His voice fell. "Listen, Burma, be careful when you walk around. I think I lost a contact lens in your place last night. Would you mind checking around the TV set?"

"Bobby, please. Can you talk?"

"What?"

"Listen, I've been thinking things over. And I think maybe I was a little hard on you last night."

"What? Oh, well, that's okay." She really shouldn't have taken that walk with Toinette, he thought. It *was* rude.

"No, it's not okay. I was plain mean. Especially after all those really deep things you said about me. Bobby, I really, really appreciate it. In fact, I started crying today thinking how nice it was."

"How nice what was?"

"About my heart and all. I've never been so touched. Listen, would you like to go get a hamburger? I'm right downstairs in the lobby."

Eddie May came walking by the desk on her way out. She mouthed a "bye-bye" to Mr. Pickens. He smiled at her, then, noticing the orange scarf around her neck, felt his feet go cold and clammy. Orange. A sickening dread crept over him.

"Bobby," Burma went on, "you know how I like to think of you like a brother . . . well, you want to know something? You got darn nice legs for a brother. I mean, like, I never did

understand incest before, used to sound so horrible and all."
She giggled.

"Donna Lee's buzzing," he lied. "I'll talk to you later. So
long."

He hung up. Sitting with his hands clasped to his head, he
tried hard not to remember. But the harder he tried, the more
he remembered. Weak with shame, he stared at the phone as it
rang steadily, urgently, right under his nose. He got up and put
on his car coat. There were stairs in back that led to an alley.
He could get out that way.

As he dragged himself down the stairway, wincing at each
prick of memory, the phone continued to ring, growing dimmer,
less harsh, step by step.

CHAPTER

Twenty-nine

When Donna Lee rang the doorbell at 517 Sweetgum, she was
still trying to recover from the trip to Moab's. The old woman's
dilapidated shotgun shack with the advertisement for Dr. Rigolet's Tonic on its side was an affront to her. She did not want
to believe that anyone in Tula Springs really *had* to live in such
squalor and misery. Not a single house on Raid Avenue was
painted, and one, a dogtrot, didn't even have a front door—
just a plastic tarp nailed to its lintel. For some reason Donna
Lee had always assumed that reality was almost everywhere
but home; she had never thought of looking for it, much less
finding it, here, practically in her own backyard.

The old woman had been wringing out clothes in the roller

of the washing machine on the porch. Standing on the orange crate that served as a front step, Donna Lee explained that her father was at a Kiwanis meeting and her mother at the beauty parlor. The old woman went on cranking the roller as if Donna Lee weren't there. Donna Lee knew she had heard her; nevertheless she repeated herself. Would she mind driving with her? There wasn't much time. The bridge party would start soon.

The roller squeaked as it cranked out a yellow frock, stiff and flat as a paper doll's dress. Donna Lee retreated a few steps into the muddy yard. She stood there a moment not knowing what to do, frozen in an awkward pose of shame and anger and civility, like one of those grinning plaster black boys that used to decorate lawns and porches. Finally, without saying a word, Donna Lee got back in her car and drove to Bishop's House of Beauty, where she informed her mother that if she wanted Moab, she would have to fetch her herself.

From the beauty parlor she drove straight to 517 Sweetgum. As she stood there waiting for someone to answer the doorbell Donna Lee felt light-headed and weak, as if some terrible hunger were gnawing at her. Yet only a few hours ago she had eaten a very substantial meal.

"Mr. Pickens isn't home."

Donna Lee looked over and saw a woman standing in the adjacent yard, a carpet of winter rye, smooth as a putting green. The woman was petite, her sagging face topped by a whirl of bright, bleached hair. In her hands were a huge pair of garden shears.

"The chubby one left just a few minutes ago," the neighbor said, crossing into the Pickenses' yard. As she leaned over to clip a withered blade from the circular patch of aspidistra, the plants' green blades cast swordlike shadows on the woman's housecoat.

"You the Keely girl?"

"Yes, ma'am," she replied, turning away. She rang again.

"Thought so. I'm Mrs. Wedge. I used to know your father, back in high school. You tell him I said hello. Tell him I was the girl sat in front of him in Miss Jesse's class."

"Yes, ma'am."

"Mercy, just look at this lawn." She clutched a handful of feathery stalks and yanked. Then, toppling a mud crawdad castle with her boyish lace-up shoes, she squished over to the cane hedge and picked up a beer can.

Rapping on the door and still receiving no answer, Donna Lee let herself into the house.

"Hello," she called out, closing the door behind her. The house smelled moldy with a sweetish, vanilla overlay. A fern drooped in the fireplace. On an end table near the love seat was a plate of chop suey and half a glass of milk.

She went to the bedroom and knocked on the door. After waiting a moment she entered.

F.X. was stretched out diagonally on the bed in his brown pajamas. The blankets were in a crumpled heap on the floor, which was littered with magazines and candy wrappers.

"Right, okay," F.X. muttered, raising his head. He rubbed his eyes. "What the hell? Who are you?" Groggily he reached for the alarm clock by the bed and looked at the illuminated dial. There were several bottles of pills and a half-empty quart of Jack Daniel's on the night table.

"I'm your brother's boss, Donna Lee Keely. We met once before."

"He's not here," he said sourly. "Just what the hell you think—"

"I came to see you."

Her hands were shaking, so she made them into fists. She had been putting off this visit for days now, always finding some excuse at the last minute not to go. But she realized that if she didn't do it today, she was a plain coward and would never get it done. And this man, who had made Mr. Pickens and Burma and Burma's friend Toinette so miserable and confused, would get off scot-free. It didn't matter that he hadn't actually committed a crime in a technical sense. In Donna Lee's eyes he was as guilty as could be. Mr. Pickens had once—the first time she had met him—been trying to get F.X. out of the house. Well, Donna Lee was determined to finish the job for him; she could not stomach bullies.

Legally, though, there was no way she could get him evicted, since the house was as much his as it was Mr. Pickens's. Nevertheless she thought she had an edge on him. Burma had told her how Mr. Pickens had beaten up F.X. Of course Donna Lee knew this was nonsense. Enraged or not, when it came to fighting, Mr. Pickens was about as effective as a guppy. No, the truth must be that someone had indeed laid into F.X., but F.X. was afraid of letting it be known. After all, he was on parole and could wind up back in Angola very easily. But for what? Well, hadn't she suspected him of being high on coke that night a few weeks ago when she had come to see Mr. Pickens about the dent? Yes, no doubt about it, F.X. was skating on very thin ice. She might not know all the details. But she knew enough to give him a good scare and make him cooperative. Hell, if he was so stuck on himself, let him go back to L.A. where he belonged.

"What do you want, lady? You just can't come barging in here like this." He switched on a lamp.

The dim yellow light showed her his face; it was not at all what she expected. In the shadows she had been seeing an extraordinarily handsome man—but the smashed nose, the bruises . . . she had no idea it was this bad.

"So Bobby beat you up," she said, trying to sound cynical,

tough. But her heart thudded violently, her palms were moist.

He groaned. "Christ, you too? I can't take any more. Where's the . . ." Some pills fell to the floor as he groped for the bourbon.

Donna Lee's throat was so tight and dry she didn't think she could talk. She reached for the shade and gave it a little pull. It shot up with a sharp clatter, knocking down a curtain rod.

"Shit!" F.X. exclaimed, grabbing his head. "What the fuck you doing?"

"I'm sorry," she mumbled, clutching the golden rod awkwardly to her chest.

The light from the window was a deep gentian-violet. Out of the corner of her eye Donna Lee saw Mrs. Wedge wielding her huge shears on a mimosa.

After taking a few swigs from the bottle, F.X. said, "What the fuck—"

"She's just pruning," Donna Lee said defensively.

"What? Who? Now, listen you, I'm giving you two seconds to get the hell out."

Donna Lee stood her ground. "I know Bobby didn't do it."

His eyes narrowed. She felt the down rise on the nape of her neck. No one had ever looked at her like that. She froze, as if a wild beast were confronting her.

"Hey, girl, it's none of your damn business, you hear?"

"I'm afraid it is."

She had never seen eyes so black, all pupil. He was breathing heavily, poised on the edge of the bed.

Without saying a word he came at her. Speechless with fright, she closed her eyes and jabbed out with the curtain rod.

"Jesus!" he cried, crumpling to the floor, his hands on his crotch.

"Oh, my God." The rod dropped with a thump.

He lay there hugging his knees to his chest.

"Did I hurt you?" she asked, kneeling beside him. "I'm so sorry. Oh, please." She was stroking his black hair.

"No, no, no more, can't take it, Jesus God help me, no more . . ."

"Shh," she said, still stroking the hair. "Everything's all right."

But everything was not all right. She was stretching out beside him, cradling him in her arms. This was not supposed to happen, she thought. Atalanta did not lie down with the boar. Everyone, even her mother, knew that.

They lay there on the dusty pine floor, mute, until his pain subsided, and hers. The only sound was of those huge shears as they bit hungrily into the living wood.

Part

THREE

"The time is at hand."
—Revelation 1:3

Thirty

Mr. Pickens and Donna Lee sat on the love seat together
drinking yaupon tea. It was Christmas Eve, and the tea was a
present from Donna Lee. Since the regular receptionist at the
law office had decided not to come back after having her baby,
Mr. Pickens was still working for Donna Lee and Mr. Herbert,
who had put up a big fuss about hiring a man permanently.
Mr. Herbert thought it was all right as an experiment, but only
as an experiment. Nevertheless, Donna Lee prevailed over
every objection, including Mr. Pickens's. Mr. Pickens was just
not sure that he liked the idea of being a receptionist. But he
hadn't been able to find another white-collar job—except for
one in Ozone, which was too far to commute to. So for the
time being he remained with Donna Lee.

During these weeks with her Mr. Pickens had lost the desire
to preach the Word to modern Baptists. In fact, he had lost all
faith in being modern, much less Baptist. The only parts of the
Gospel that he believed in now were the bad parts, like the
time Jesus was hungry and the fig tree, which he cursed, had
no fruit. The rest was nothing but a story. After all, if there
was a good God, a loving God, would He have treated Mr.
Pickens so badly? He hadn't asked for much out of life, just
the chance to love someone with his whole heart and soul—
and now this was denied him. Toinette wouldn't even speak to
him.

Most of the time now he was angry in a quiet, sullen way.
Mr. Herbert, mistaking this anger for a nascent backbone,

became reconciled to Mr. Pickens's presence in the office. In fact Mr. Pickens began to show a particular aptitude for legal work that neither the former receptionist nor Eddie May, the secretary, could perform. With little guidance he soon learned how to summarize lengthy depositions and research precedents in the library. Motivated by his strong sense of right and wrong, he took a personal interest in each case and was only a nuisance when he decided on his own that one of Donna Lee's or Mr. Herbert's clients was in the wrong. His most recent assignment was the class-action suit that the residents of Raid Avenue, stirred up by Donna Lee, were preparing against the city. It was this suit that she and Mr. Pickens were discussing on the love seat.

"Did Moab sign the complaint?" Donna Lee asked, gazing at the Christmas tree, a loblolly she had chopped down, without permission, on Mayor Binwanger's land near the creosote plant.

Mr. Pickens shrugged.

"Well, didn't you explain, Carl? Didn't you tell her about the garbage collection and the sewer repairs and the paving, all the good things we could get for them?"

Mr. Pickens had instructed everyone to call him Carl. After all, that was his name, Carl Robert. He was sick to death of Bobby. Lighting his cigarette—this was something he had just taken up for no other reason than that he felt like it, and to hell with cancer—he said, "She wanted to see my shoe catalog."

"What?"

"I used to sell shoes once. Mrs. Wedge has got her all fired up about the shoes I used to sell."

"Well, for Christ's sake, show it to her."

"I can't. I burned it."

They sat for a moment, silently, as the Christmas-tree lights blinked on and off. Donna Lee bit a nail, her blue eyes focused on the stained-glass window. Like a clock pendulum, F.X.'s foot would swing into view, then disappear, a wing-shaped shadow darkening the leaded panes. He was out on the porch swing, in one of his moods, which meant that everyone was supposed to leave him alone for a while.

The second operation on F.X.'s nose had been a big success. Mr. Pickens couldn't tell the difference between the original F.X. and the revamped version. But F.X. could. He said his face was ruined, and that was that. He had a job now as the host of a fancy plantation restaurant over in the next parish. They dressed him up in white tie and tails and encouraged him to sound foreign to the guests. The pay was excellent, and he was a big hit. Most of the time he didn't complain about Far Oaks—that was the name of the plantation—and seemed happy enough with the job. But sometimes he got in one of his moods, and no one, not even Donna Lee, could do anything with him. He would sit for hours by himself, usually out back under the mimosa, nursing a bottle of Jack Daniel's.

At one time it had looked as if F.X. and Donna Lee were going to move to Ozone, where they planned to fix up a lake-front house that used to belong to an aunt of hers. But then at the last minute F.X. changed his mind. He said it was too big a commitment to make this early on in the game. Donna Lee did not seem too disappointed. In fact Mr. Pickens suspected her of being almost relieved. Although she spent a great deal of time at the house on Sweetgum, she kept her clothes and belongings in her own apartment, traipsing back across the ditch each morning to wash up and dress properly for the office. Mr. Pickens had never seen anyone look so radiant and exhausted at the same time; it reminded him of a movie he had once seen, years ago, about this foreign girl who was sickly and had sore knees and kept on seeing this lady hover-ing over a rosebush. Once or twice he had come upon Donna Lee weeping silently as she stir-fried supper in the wok, and he would be embarrassed. If ever two people were wrong for each other, it was F.X. and Donna Lee. They both freely admitted it to Mr. Pickens. But neither one could do anything about it. They were violently in love.

"Donna Lee, I got you your present," Mr. Pickens said, handing her an envelope.

"How sweet," she said, pecking him on the cheek. She opened it. Inside was a card, SEASON'S GREETINGS, and inside the card was a check for $187.22, the cost of the repairs on her Volvo. Mr. Pickens still knew he was innocent, but he decided to pay it anyway, since he couldn't stand the idea of going to court. Besides, Donna Lee had given him a raise at work, and she had scrubbed the kitchen floor last week.

"And here's my present to you," she said, tearing up the check. "I never really cared about the money, Bobby . . . Carl. All that mattered was that you admitted you were wrong. Thank you."

She wiped away a tear.

Mr. Pickens coughed into his fist genteelly.

"I really wish you'd come to the party tonight," she said. Behind the stained glass the shadow hovered, disappeared. "We need you to help out with the kids."

Donna Lee had organized a Christmas party at Josie Wayne, the first step in her campaign to reopen the recreation center for the whole town, blacks and whites alike. Burma was moving out, temporarily staying at Donna Lee's until she could find an apartment of her own in town. She had helped Donna Lee solicit contributions for Josie Wayne. Donna Lee's father got the Kiwanis Club to fork over three hundred and fifty dollars, Mr. Dambar made a private contribution of a thousand dollars (Donna Lee had played his guilt just right), and

Mr. Binwanger promised that when he was elected mayor he would provide funds for repairs and upkeep. Donna Lee and Burma had been shopping for days, not knowing how many people to expect for the party. It had made her very edgy.

"Well, Bobby?"

"Carl." Mr. Pickens stubbed out his Lucky Strike. "I have other plans."

"It's Emmet, isn't it? You're afraid of Emmet."

Mr. Pickens tapped out another cigarette from the soft pack. The other day, while he was buying F.X. a six-pack at Dr. Henry's, Emmet had accosted him in the potato chip aisle and threatened to smash in his tin head—that's what he had said, tin head—unless he stopped fooling around with his fiancée. Mr. Pickens assured him that he hadn't the slightest interest in his fiancée—in fact, ever since that drunken night at Josie Wayne, he had gone out of his way to avoid seeing or even speaking with her—but this only seemed to make Emmet madder. He picked up a cylinder of Pringle's and swatted Mr. Pickens on the elbow. The manager, a burly man, threw Emmet out, then let Mr. Pickens exit by the back door.

"Emmet?" Mr. Pickens said, inhaling deeply. "Oh, you mean the guy Burma's engaged to?"

"Come off it. Now, listen, you have nothing to worry about. Burma told me this afternoon, she's through with him. She's called off the whole thing. There isn't going to be a wedding."

Mr. Pickens failed to hide his alarm.

"Now what? I just told you, he's not going to be there tonight. And if he shows up and makes a scene, F.X.'ll beat the shit out of him. So you have to come, Carl. Really, you have no excuse."

"But why did she—I mean, the invitations, didn't they already go out?"

"To the wedding, those invitations? No. She never did mail

them. Burma's been doing a lot of thinking these days. We've talked a lot about Emmet, what he means to her. She did like him an awful lot. He was very good for her in his own way. You realize that before Emmet she was a virgin? Now, don't you dare tell her I told you this. I really shouldn't be talking, but—"

"Don't, then."

"What? But anyway, Emmet really taught Burma a lot about her body, about being a woman. She really is a very sensual person"—she paused, giving him a casual glance—"really in tune with herself now, but you see, we figured out that sex was not enough. She has to have more in her life, something really solid and . . . Christ, Bobby, do you have to smoke those filthy things?" She waved the smoke from her face. He held his cigarette at arm's length.

"I'm going to take a shower," he said, standing up.

"Does that mean you're coming?"

"I told you. I have plans."

"Bobby, after all the work I've done, you have no idea—"

"Carl," he snapped, going into the hall.

When he had got out of the shower and was drying himself, he overheard Donna Lee and F.X. talking softly in the bedroom.

"You going to be all right?"

"It's gone now. I'll make it."

"F.X., what is it? What happens to you?"

"Nothing—just this black hole. I was thinking about Mom, that funeral I never got to go to."

"Oh, baby, my baby boy. Come here."

"I'm sorry, really. Oh, Lord, I love you, I love you so much."

"No, F.X. Not now. We're late, please. Shhh. Come on, get dressed. Shhhh."

"Is he ready yet?"

"He's not coming."

"What?"

"It's my fault. I'm too pushy. If I could just keep my big mouth shut. I know he thinks I'm trying to shove him and Burma together."

"Well, you are, aren't you?"

"No. Not anymore. It's wrong. I just hate people who do things like that. It's disgusting. Besides, it wasn't just because of Bobby she split up with Emmet. I always make it sound like it was."

"She split up?"

"For good. Here's your other sock. Yeah, her mother couldn't be happier. Of course she's trying to get Burma to come live with her again, but Burma's been pretty good about it . . . really stood up to her. Oh, F.X., put something on underneath."

"Too hot, no. Say, darling, what if she really was in love with Emmet?"

"What? Oh, don't be silly. Now, here, sweetie, that's right, stick your little arm through the hole. Okay. Really, F.X., I don't know what makes you say such stupid things."

"What?"

"Forget it."

CHAPTER

Thirty-one

Mr. Keely answered the door wearing a blue sash around his middle. After shaking Mr. Pickens's hand vigorously and proclaiming how wonderful Mr. Pickens was looking and asking where he got that wonderful tie, Mr. Keely ushered him into the living room, where Mrs. Keely, dressed in an elegant silk gown, offered him some divinity on a silver salver. Munching the candy, Mr. Pickens settled into a worn leather chair while Mr. Keely went into the kitchen for eggnog.

With an uncertain smile in his general direction Mrs. Keely commented on how warm it was for Christmas. Mr. Pickens agreed, then tried hard to think of something interesting to say. The situation was a little awkward. Mr. and Mrs. Keely were not going to the party at Josie Wayne because Mrs. Keely couldn't bear the thought of actually seeing that man, much less spending Christmas Eve with him. She had told Donna Lee that F.X. was a sword in her side. Donna Lee pleaded with her to at least meet him before she passed judgment, but Mrs. Keely said she didn't need to pass judgment on him. Society had already done it for her when they put him in jail.

Mr. Pickens had heard all this from Donna Lee and was anxious now to assure Mrs. Keely that, one, he had nothing to do with F.X. and Donna Lee's falling in love and, two, he disapproved of the relationship himself. But he didn't know quite how to bring the subject up. And he wasn't sure that it was appropriate to comment on it now, anyway. His main concern was to make a good impression on the Keelys, whom he wanted to cultivate as friends. They had class, these people, real class.

Mr. Keely returned with two crystal cups of eggnog. With a courtly nod of the head he handed one to his wife and the other to Mr. Pickens. Adjusting the crease in his trousers— he was wearing his best suit—Mr. Pickens wondered if Donna Lee knew how lucky she was to have such a gentleman for a father. His own father, Mr. Pickens senior, had to be waited on hand and foot.

"Come over here, Dad," Mrs. Keely said, picking up a pair of pliers from a mahogany end table.

When Mr. Keely was standing in front of her chair, she yanked on the zipper of the blue sash with the pliers, but it didn't budge.

"Moab, our maid, gave Mr. Keely this reducing belt for Christmas," she said as she tugged. Her white hair and blue eyes entranced Mr. Pickens. She was so lovely, really extraordinary. "I do wish she had saved her money."

"It must be the wrong size—a little tight," Mr. Keely said. "Careful, Ann."

"Hold still." Her tongue between her teeth, she yanked again with both hands. The pliers clattered to the floor.

"Oh," she said in a faraway voice, her blue eyes welling up with tears. "Please excuse me, Mr. Pickens."

She got up, unhurried, and walked calmly into the next room.

"We're so glad you could drop by tonight," Mr. Keely said, his eyes fixed on the swinging door she had walked through.

"Is something the matter?"

Mr. Keely hummed as he tugged at the zipper of the reducing belt. "What? Oh, no, fine, fine, everything's fine. Hmmmm

. . . Christmas Eve, you know." He sighed. "First year we ever had it without Donna Lee. I guess Ann's taking it pretty hard. Yes, well, have some more divinity, sir. Fine. You'll pardon me a moment, I hope?" Hunched over a little—he was quite tall and hefty—he shambled into the other room.

Mr. Pickens got out a cigarette and lit it, then walked over to the baby grand. Inhaling the smoke deep into his lungs, he idly thumbed through the John Thompson instruction book lying on the bench. "Dance of the Hours" was marked with violet ink: *Count! F# please, ma'am! Legato here, Ann! Wrist down!* What were they saying back there in the kitchen? he wondered. Should he go? It was odd, but Mr. Pickens thought Mrs. Keely had seemed surprised to see him when he first walked in. Yet hadn't Mr. Keely told him last week in the law office that he could drop by anytime during the holidays? Maybe he should have phoned first, though, and made it more formal.

A muffled sob came from behind the swinging door. Dismayed, Mr. Pickens retreated to the far corner of the living room, where he picked a book at random from the shelf. After gazing at a picture of the spleen for a few moments, he flipped the pages to a highly magnified photograph of human skin. It looked like the surface of a forbidden planet, a craggy, inhospitable terrain with monstrous creatures lurking in the crevasses. According to the book, no matter how clean you were—they loved warm showers—these microscopic beasts considered your skin their home and thrived. There was even an entirely separate species that inhabited the flesh at the base of the eyelashes. Mr. Pickens felt his throat tighten. If we really could see, he thought, if we really knew what we were embracing, could we actually desire anyone? This, after all, was what Toinette was really like, up close. She was no different when it came right down to it. Closing his eyes, Mr.

Pickens tried hard to make himself believe that she was this repulsive and . . .

"More eggnog?"

Mr. Pickens blushed as if he had been caught with a dirty book. Mr. Keely had returned, still encumbered by his gift.

"Uh, maybe I should be going," Mr. Pickens said, hoping Mr. Keely would protest and insist that he stay. He had nowhere else to go.

"Yes, of course, I understand," Mr. Keely said, going to the front door and opening it.

Not knowing what else to do, Mr. Pickens followed him. Outside it had begun to grow dark, yet there was still so much time left: it was barely five thirty. "Say, Mr. Keely," he said, standing half in the door, half out, "maybe if you just stepped out of it, sort of slid it down your legs."

"The belt? Hey, great idea. Well, have a good time now, hear?"

A vague panic gripped Mr. Pickens. "Actually, sir, if it's all right with you, I'd really like to—"

"Sure, sure." Mr. Keely winked, patted him on the shoulder, then gave him a definite nudge out the door. "You go ahead, sounds like it'll be a fine party out there."

"No, I—"

"Merry Christmas, Bobby."

"Carl," Mr. Pickens said to the door that was shut in his face. He stood there a moment, then walked away from the house. In the bleary dusk everything—the hydrangeas along the brick path to the driveway, the fig sapling guyed against a possible wind, the wheelbarrow filled with mulch—seemed distant and unreal.

CHAPTER
Thirty-two

Waiting for the traffic light by City Hall, Mr. Pickens wondered if maybe instead of going on to Sweetgum he should turn left and head out on the Old Jefferson Davis Highway for the nursing home. He wouldn't have to stay long, just long enough to say hello to his mother; it would ease his conscience. And besides, the trip up and back would eat up some time.

He turned left.

Just outside the city limits was the Sugar Shack. Mr. Pickens passed the neon sign, then braked hard and backed up into the parking area. He was furious at himself. Why should he turn himself into Mr. Ames for her? If she wanted to flirt, let her flirt with the real Mr. Ames. It was degrading. Would Mrs. Keely ever do such a thing to her daughter? Mrs. Keely could be a hundred and ten and she'd never behave that way. There were limits, after all.

He got out of the car and ordered a banana split to tide him over until supper. While the girl made it—he was the only customer—he walked over to the wading pool where the alligator was chained up. The alligator was supposed to attract tourists who were going to see the plantations in the next parish. A few pennies were lodged on the alligator's dark hide, and a Dentyne wrapper clung to its snout. Mr. Pickens leaned on the fence that surrounded the pool of filthy green water and stared vacantly at the beast, waiting for it to move. He kicked the Cyclone fence, hoping this would rouse it, but it continued to just lie there, as still and bloated as death.

"Pick up number twelve," the loudspeaker blared.

He kicked the fence again. The dreams came back to him now in which he would be forced (by whom? what?) to swim past alligators that were lurking, half submerged, in Tula Creek. Donna Lee told him these were about sex, which made him quit telling her his dreams. He didn't want to sound abnormal to her. F.X., though, didn't seem to mind. She and F.X. would go on for hours about their dreams, not the least bit embarrassed.

"Hey, you, white man—number twelve!"

Mr. Pickens looked up and saw the girl gesturing to him. He looked at the stub in his hand: number 12.

"One sixty-eight," she said, shoving the banana split through the plastic window. She was young, thirteen, maybe fourteen. Her skin was very pink, an unhealthy, rashlike pink, but otherwise, with her short kinky hair and wide nose and lips, she looked black to him. A red Santa sleigh held one of her pigtails in place.

He took the banana split to the picnic table by the alligator pool. The fluorescent light flickering above him gave a greenish cast to his skin, which he gazed at a moment—the skin of his hand—before lifting the spoon to his mouth. Finally he took a bite of ice cream and discovered he couldn't eat.

Whatever hope he had had of something ever developing between him and Toinette had been spoiled when Donna Lee took up with F.X. Mr. Pickens had tried to explain that he had had nothing to do with it, but Toinette wouldn't listen. She was sure he had conspired against her. Then she told him she had never liked him in the first place; the only reason she let him go out with her was to make F.X. jealous. Mr. Pickens

told her he knew that—he always knew that, or at least suspected it—but it didn't matter. He told her it was just impossible someone could love someone the way he did and the
other person wouldn't feel it after a while. All he needed was
time, time for her to get to know him, to see how full his
heart was. He was sure that if he was given just half a chance,
she would see how real his love was, how happy it would
make her.

That's why he always carried the watch around with him
wherever he went. He had bought the watch at the mall in
Mississippi, bought it on time, the only way he could afford
it, with payments stretching out for the next two years. It
was far better than the watch he had stolen from her and
thrown into Tula Creek. He knew that if only he could find
a way to give it to her, if only she could see the sparkling
diamonds—they were real!—her heart would soften.

He had tried calling at her house with the watch, but
Toinette, who was home from St. Jude for the holidays,
wouldn't come out of her bedroom. Mrs. Quaid wouldn't let
him leave the gift there, either. She said the only Christmas
present they needed from him was a promise that he and his
filthy brother would pack up and leave town for good. That
same evening he had seen Toinette at Junior's sitting in a
booth with a big good-looking guy in a St. Jude varsity
letter jacket. They were holding hands, and he was nuzzling
her neck. Mr. Pickens had to leave; he couldn't stand the
sight. Then just today he had seen her going into Sonny
Boy, or at least he thought it was she. He was a block away
and ran as fast as he could to the store. While he was search-
ing for her Mr. Randy waylaid him. He was worked up about
something as usual and asked Mr. Pickens about an order of
place mats that had been shipped months ago from Atlanta.
They were lost, and he was trying to pin the blame on Mr.

Pickens, who had the satisfaction of telling him that he and his fucking place mats could go straight to hell. But that was the only satisfaction he enjoyed, for he never did find Toinette in the store.

He felt the watch case in the breast pocket of his suit. The gum wrapper on the alligator's snout stirred as a soft April-like breeze wafted over from the pasture across the highway.

"Fool," he said, taking the watch case out and holding it in his hand. "You damn fool."

The girl with the sleigh in her hair was leaning on her elbows gazing at the highway, her face slack, hopeless, a little sour. When she saw him approach—he had a peculiar look on his face—her chapped lips tightened with fear and distrust.

"Here," he said, shoving the velvet watch case under the plastic window. "Merry Christmas."

Before she could say anything, he hurried to his car. There, he thought as he started the engine. It was done.

And time, which Mr. Pickens could neither steal nor buy, that infernal, unrelenting dance of the hours, so graceless, so mechanical, so cuckoo—he wanted no part of it anymore. He was through, finished.

The ditch was too steep, almost a canal, and the telephone poles were on the other side of it. He rode on, waiting for the ditch to level out a little so he could aim the car at one of those poles. It would look like an accident, a typical holiday statistic. There would be liquor on his breath—he had brought along a flask of bourbon and diet Dr Pepper, stashing it in the glove compartment—and that would explain everything. Too much celebrating.

There was no moon yet, and the stars were veiled by high, thin clouds that domed a huge coliseum of night. The ditch seemed to be getting shallower. He pressed down on the accelerator and took a swig from the flask. When he was a kid, there was a gang of boys on Sweetgum he wanted to belong to, but to belong you had to eat a tar bubble off a telephone pole. The poles oozed tar—creosote actually—in summer. He had got as far as putting his tongue to the bubble, but that alone was enough to make him retch. He never did eat one. Mr. Pickens remembered this as the poles whipped by the yellow Chevette. He was going so fast they almost seemed to bend a little, like frail saplings in a breeze.

Just where a series of old, faded Burma Shave signs began, the ditch became shallow enough to cross. He pressed the accelerator to the floor. But even though he kept his foot down hard, the car gradually slowed until finally, at the punch line sign, where he planned to swing off the road, he was hardly moving at all. Mystified, he got out and looked under the hood with a flashlight. He knew nothing about engines, but he looked anyway. After jiggling a wire he slammed the hood shut and got back inside to try to start the car. Then it dawned on him; the gas gauge was on empty.

With a great deal of effort he was able to shove the car to the side of the road, down which, in the distance, two headlights shone. He crossed the asphalt road and waved the flashlight in an arc, but then, as the car approached, he switched off the light and hurried back to his car. He had changed his mind. He didn't want some red-neck picking him up. Lord only knew what these farmers were like out here.

The car turned out to be a pickup with a fancy camper stuck on behind the cab. A woman in a white cowboy hat peered suspiciously at him, rolling up her window as she eased by. He had the car radio on and pretended to be absorbed by the music.

He couldn't be that far from Miss Mina's, he figured. Maybe

a half mile or so. After locking the car he started to trek beside the highway. A steady insect hum, like a refrigerator's, came from the pasture on the other side of a barbed-wire fence. He stumbled over a dried cow patty, then quickened his pace when he heard a dog howling in the distance. Although it was still warm, the breeze had stiffened, making the speed-limit sign he passed creak loudly. Whenever headlights blared across his face he tried to look mean so no one would stop.

Miss Mina had a manger scene set up in her front yard. The three kings, the shepherd, and the Mary and Joseph were just about life-size, but the cow—or maybe it was an ox—seemed to have come from a different manger scene, since it was the size of a small dog. Near the baby was a lamb with a light bulb inside its stomach. One of its ears was broken off.

With a sigh Mr. Pickens walked up to the compact blue house. He would ask for gas, and that would be it. Nothing else. Nothing. Lord, it was Christmas Eve—how could he even think of such a thing?

He rang the doorbell.

Why not, though? After all, he didn't believe anymore. What difference did it make? This was a night just like any other, wasn't it?

The porch light went on. The door opened.

Emmet Orney stood there in his undershorts, dark and skinny as a starving native. They gaped at each other. Then, with a little cry from the back of his throat, Emmet tore out after Mr. Pickens, who was already fleeing across the yard. Emmet caught up with him near the manger, where they both tumbled to the ground. The shepherd fell first, then the black king with the myrrh smashed against the lamb. As Mr.

Pickens and Emmet rolled over and over, struggling silently, fiercely, like Jacob and the man, the clouds so high above them melted, and the stars shone forth in hundred-carat glory.

CHAPTER

Thirty-three

The vaulting horse at Josie Wayne had a moose head attached to one end and a red flannel blanket draped over its middle. Donna Lee, who had been pouring Mr. Randy a glass of punch, hurried over to the moose and snatched some matches out of a child's hand. "Now, why do you want to burn Santa's reindeer?" she asked the little boy, who had been holding a flame to the moose's ear.

Whirling about, the child fled across the basketball court to Moab. The old woman was sitting in a corner by herself next to the sumac, which had been decorated with popcorn and tinsel. She was the only black adult to show up at the party, bringing with her five great-nieces and -nephews. As for the white people, neither Mr. Dambar nor Mr. Binwanger had bothered to make an appearance. In fact the only towns-people who had shown up, besides a group of Burma's co-workers from Sonny Boy, who stayed about five minutes, were Mrs. Jenks, Dr. McFlug, and Mr. Randy. Mr. Randy had had a bitter argument with his wife during the first five minutes of the party—they had arrived early—and she had left by herself.

"What are you going to do with all this food?" Mrs. Jenks

asked as she put on her cloth coat with the mink collar. It was only 7:30, and she was leaving.

"I'm so glad you could come," Donna Lee replied, trying to hide her annoyance. On the counters were mounds of chicken salad sandwiches cut into little squares without the crusts. Bowls of fresh carrots, cauliflower, peppers, and cherry tomatoes with special dips were distributed about the room, along with potato chips and cookies. In the refrigerator were six quarts of Hawaiian Punch that hadn't even been opened.

"If you ask me, it's a sin," Mrs. Jenks said, shaking her head. She was a very broad woman, whose stiffly permed white hair had a bluish tint. Pinned to her breast was a poinsettia corsage, which drooped on a broken stem. "Folks in Tula Springs ought to be ashamed of themselves. I'm going to give them a piece of my mind next week, in my column."

Donna Lee felt a sudden surge of warmth for her. Perhaps, after all, she had been too hasty in condemning her. "Mrs. Jenks, I wish you would stay," she said, patting her tentatively on the sleeve.

"Mr. Ray's got to have his Christmas, honey. He's waiting on me back home."

"Please give him my love," Donna Lee said, not looking the old woman in the eye. Ever since making out Mrs. Jenks's handyman's will, Donna Lee had planned on visiting him regularly. She knew Mr. Ray was lonely and in pain. But somehow she had never got around to it. There was always so much work to do.

"Scaredy-cats, that's what they are," Mrs. Jenks said, thumping her cane on the floor. "The doctor himself has come out, a bona fide medical authority. You think he'd be here if it wasn't safe?"

Donna Lee frowned. "Safe? Mrs. Jenks, what could possibly be dangerous out here?"

"That's what I say. But our dear fellow citizens, they get themselves worked into a dither by the Baton Rouge papers and all those shows on TV."

Distracted by the loud music, Donna Lee called over her shoulder to Burma, asking her to turn it down a little. "I'm sorry, Mrs. Jenks," she said, leaning closer to her. "What were you saying?"

"Dear, look at the time. I really got to be going. Who's that colored woman over there? Maybe I should say something to her before I leave."

"That's Mrs. Johnson, Moab Johnson. She's a wonderful woman."

"I'll say hello, then."

While Mrs. Jenks plowed through a game of jacks three girls were playing on the floor Donna Lee went over to the record player and turned down the volume herself. The Christmas carols Burma had brought were all sung by Walt Disney creatures, mice and chipmunks and grasshoppers, and it was terribly obnoxious.

"Oh, Burma," Donna Lee said to her friend, who was carrying a tray of drinks. "Listen, is F.X. ready?" He was going to appear as Santa Claus, bringing some toys for the children.

"I haven't seen him," Burma said, putting down the tray. She had had her hair teased and streaked at the beauty college, ruining the natural look Donna Lee had labored over.

"Hon, don't give Mr. Randy any more to drink. I think he's tight."

They both looked over at him standing beside Mrs. Jenks, who had just finished shaking Moab's hand and was turning to leave. Donna Lee heard Mr. Randy make a crack about Mrs. Jenks to Moab as the old white lady shuffled toward the door, poking her cane at anything that got in her way, which included the sumac and Dr. McFlug. Moab smiled and said something to Mr. Randy, who looked slightly walleyed.

Donna Lee was indignant. After all the work she had done, not just for Raid Avenue but on this party itself, Moab still wouldn't speak to her. And yet here she was chatting it up with a drunken stranger.

"What's wrong with you tonight?" Burma asked.

"Nothing."

"You been acting crabby."

"How in the hell can I be happy when no one showed up? Even Mrs. Jenks thinks it's a disgrace. And by the way, you haven't exactly been the life of the party yourself. If I were you, Burma, I'd stop looking at the door every two seconds. Bobby isn't coming, and that's that."

Burma's eyes went bright with anger. "It's still early—how do you know?"

Donna Lee took her hand and pressed it. "Hon, you're not being realistic about this. Remember what I told you yesterday—you've got to learn not to put all your hopes in other people. You've got to learn how to be happy with yourself and stop—"

"And stop listening to other people," Burma said, wrenching her hand free. "That's right, girl, you told me yourself I had to stop listening to everyone else and do what I thought right. Well, now I'm doing it. I'm telling you to bug off. I'm tired of your advice, hear? 'Cause no matter what you say, miss, you're not going to make me give up hoping. I'll stare at that door as much as I want, understand?" Folding her arms across her chest, Burma turned away from Donna Lee and glared at the door.

Feeling miffed and awkward, Donna Lee stood there a

moment trying to think of something to say. So this was the thanks she got for being a friend, she thought. Well, if Burma wanted to be left alone, she'd leave her alone.

"Are y'all having a good time?" With a tight smile on her face Donna Lee had walked over to Moab and Mr. Randy. Moab hugged her varsity football sweater as if she felt a sudden chill.

"Fruitcake's good," Mr. Randy replied, his mouth half filled with crumbs. One of the stays of his clip-on tie had worked loose from his collar.

"Would you like some fruitcake, Mrs. Johnson?"

Moab kept her face averted.

"Mrs. Johnson?"

"I don't think she likes fruitcake," Mr. Randy said, moving off toward the counter.

"Is that true?" Donna Lee persisted. She squatted so that she was face to face with the old woman. "Maybe you'd like something else."

The old woman's freckled face remained impassive.

"Talk to me, Mrs. Johnson," Donna Lee said, surprised at her own vehemence, which was barely disguised. "Talk to me."

The old woman's eyes were fixed on the sumac, an arm's length away. Her eyes became lustrous, even blacker, as she whispered to the shrub, "I seen a woman sit upon a scarlet-colored beast, and upon her forehead was a name written . . ."

"What?" Donna Lee said, not sure she was hearing right. She leaned closer. "What are you saying? I don't understand."

Moab turned to her, and for the first time their eyes met. "I talked, girl. That's what you done asked. I talked what was in my heart."

"But tell me, what does it mean?"

"You's scared, girl," she said in a soft voice. "Why you so

scared of this old lady here? Moab, she just a straw in the wind." She brushed a piece of lint off Donna Lee's sweater. "You don't ever feel that wind, do you, girl? When you feel it, child, you don't have to worry no more about nobody." Calmly, deliberately, Moab reached out and swatted a nephew, who was eating the popcorn decorations off the sumac.

"Mrs. Johnson, I still don't— What?" she said, feeling someone tap her on the shoulder. It was Dr. McFlug.

"I got to be on my way, Miss Keely. Velmarae, my wife, is having a few people over tonight."

Donna Lee stood up. "I'm so glad you could come, Dr. McFlug."

His long white face looked sorrowful. "More people should have come," he said, patting the pockets of his checked overcoat, which bulged with sandwiches she had seen him purloin earlier that evening.

"Yes, Mrs. Jenks was saying . . ." Donna Lee remembered something that was bothering her. "Dr. McFlug, why would people be scared?"

"Scared?"

"Mrs. Jenks said some people might think it wasn't safe out here. How could they possibly think that?"

"Ah, yes. Good question. Those barrels are buried six feet under in containers that simply can't rust open. It's all scientifically safe, absolutely nothing to be concerned over."

"Barrels? What are you talking about?"

Dr. McFlug's spindly frame seemed to sway ever so slightly. "Why, the barrels out back, right behind the hall."

"Not . . . no, it couldn't be. This, here, Dr. McFlug, this isn't the dump?"

For the first time in her life Donna Lee saw Dr. McFlug smile. "Aren't you cute," he said fondly, patting her on the arm. "Well, must get going. Give my best to your father."

A little black girl wearing shorts and a halter top clung to Dr. McFlug's leg. He reached into his pocket and pulled out a peppermint stick, which she jammed into her mouth and sucked on while riding his shoes to the door. He waved good-bye as he was going out, but Donna Lee, who was looking at him, did not register the wave. Tula Springs was burying the new, legalized toxic wastes here, right here at Josie Wayne, and she was trying to turn the whole place into a playground. She had even sat through a Sierra Club meeting that discussed this issue, and yet at the time it had never occurred to her to ask exactly where they planned to bury the waste chemicals. What was the matter with her?

"Hey, Donna Lee, look at this girl—she's really something," Mr. Randy said, sweat pouring down his face. He was sparring with the biggest niece, who was landing some interesting punches on the store manager's belly. The smaller girls were trying to toss a volleyball through the basketball net.

"Donna Lee," Mr. Randy called out again. "Look."

But she walked right past them with a faint smile, out the front door. She needed a few moments alone to collect herself.

As she stood on the porch letting her eyes adjust to the dark the little boy who had been eating the popcorn off the sumac suddenly poked his round head out a window and, pointing a finger at her, called out in a shrill voice, "Misery! Hey, you, Misery!" He stuck out his tongue. "Baby the Great! Baby the Great!" he chanted until an arm appeared and yanked him inside.

Donna Lee stumbled over a seesaw as she hurried down to the riverbank. The moon was just rising, an ivory, gibbous moon that frosted a sandspit on the far shore. She picked her way through the undergrowth that fringed the bank until the grating sound of the mice's carols in the hall became mercifully dim. A few feet ahead was a clay mound, big as a boulder, on the water's edge. She rested there, hugging her knees to her chest.

Suddenly, instead of being soothed by the river's murmur and the lonely sweep of river birch silvered in the pale light, her heart began racing. She was being watched, studied. Rising slowly, she looked about her. There was no sign of anyone; the woods were still, not a leaf stirred. She got off the mound, which had begun to seem too conspicuous. *"Echoing their joyous strains . . ."* the mice sang as she got closer to the hall. She paused, worried that she was making too much noise. How silly, she scolded herself—but remained motionless. Then taking a cautious step forward, she saw it, the red, something red with a long tail half in the river, on whose black surface were scattered shards of light, dim as the distant stars.

"Why didn't you say something?" she demanded. "I walked right by you, you could have said hello."

F.X. sat on the log, a whitish, barkless sycamore that trailed into the water. He had on his Santa Claus outfit, a pillow stuffed beneath the wide belt, but he held the beard in his hands.

"I thought you saw me," he said in a flat voice.

"You think if I saw you I'd walk right on by?"

He remained silent.

"Well?" She leaned against a nearby tree. "Oh, I see. You're in one of your moods."

"Go away."

"Your mother, huh? Or is it your father this time? How he hurt your feelings, how he screwed you up, huh?"

F.X. tossed a stone into the water. "Christ."

"No, not your father? Then maybe it's Elizabeth. You're brooding over all those injustices, right? She gave you the shaft, really did you in. And Ora too, and Charlene—oh, God,

I'm so tried of hearing how poor, innocent F.X. was mistreated by all those horrible people. I am tired of it, you hear— sick to death. Your mother, your father, all your ex-wives, your girl friends, the jury, the cops—you've been screwed by everyone, haven't you, F.X.?"

"Get out," he muttered, turning away.

"No wonder the idea of rape appealed to you. I never could figure out this rape thing. I always thought it was so bizarre that a man could come up with a plan like that. But now I see it. It's as natural as can be. You want to get screwed, you want everyone to screw you, Toinette, me, Bobby, just so you'll have an excuse. I'm a failure because *they* did this to me. Oh, I get it now, F.X. I get it. You never really believed Toinette would go along with you in the first place. That's why you picked her. You knew she was scared, you *knew* she was bound to blab and screw things up. You were never serious about your little plan, were you? You stalled, just waiting for someone else to make a mistake. All that time Bobby was staying at the LaSteeles', you did nothing. And it would have been so easy to find him. Any half-ass could have found him, a couple blocks from your own house. But no, you needed an excuse not to go ahead. Then finally you got your wish. Toinette screwed up the whole thing. She betrayed you. It's *her* fault now that you're not famous, not a stupid pinhead celebrity."

"*Sweetly singing o'er the plains*," the tinny voices sang in the distance where the warm, yellow light shone from the hall windows.

"And now," Donna Lee went on, "now you're planning to blame me. You're trying to think of some way to blame me for our love falling apart. How can I get out of it, how can I run away and make it look like she screwed me?" Donna Lee kicked a fallen branch out of the way. "Well, honey, let me tell you something. I'm not letting you do it. I'm going to keep on loving you good and hard. You're not going to have the slightest excuse this time. It's going to be your fault, *entirely* your fault."

"Sure, babe, my fault," F.X. said, suddenly getting up off the log. His pillow-stuffed belly sagged as he took a step toward her. "It's all my fault. Now you can go with a clear conscience: I take all the blame. Hell, I've known all along it would never work out. You're just too good for me, aren't you? I mean, yeah, maybe F.X. is all right for a little fling, huh? That's okay, 'cause you feel sorry for him, don't you? He's nothing but a two-bit jailbird."

"F.X., don't."

"Sure, that's about as close to love as you'll ever come—feeling sorry for someone. You look down your nose at me just the way you look down your nose at them." He pointed toward the hall. "It's all a farce, a fucking farce. I can't tell you how sick it made me to see you patronizing everyone tonight—Burma, Miss Jenks, Moab, everyone. Maybe they don't see it, but I do. And I've had it. So take your little toys and stuff them—" He threw the burlap sack of toys at her and started to walk away.

Donna Lee's fists clenched. One of the toys in the bag had knocked a front tooth, and it hurt something awful. "Goddammit, come back here!"

She ran a few steps and clawed at the red velveteen material on his back. "Take it off."

"What?"

"Give me that suit, the pillow. If you're too chickenshit to do it, then let me." She yanked at the belt.

He flung the beard to the ground and began unbuttoning the jacket.

"Glo-o-o-o-o-o-o-o-o-o-o-o-o-o-o-o-ria, in excelsis Deo!"

After he unzipped the red pants, she grabbed the pillow from his stomach and held it to her own, waiting for him to step out of the pants. All he had on underneath was his bikini briefs.

"Ruin the poor children's Christmas," she said angrily as she pulled the pants on over her skirt. The pillow dropped into one wide leg. "Christ, F.X., could you help, please! Hold the fucking pillow. I can't do everything."

Naked except for his boots and briefs, he stood behind her with his arms around her waist, holding the pillow in place.

"Now what am I supposed to do like this?" he said into her ear. She was having trouble fastening the belt over the pillow.

"I told you to wear something underneath, didn't I?"

"Angels we have heard on high . . ."

"What's wrong with this belt, F.X.? Did you break the buckle?"

"Here, let me."

"No, now the pillow's sliding down. Keep still."

"Watch it, that's my finger—shit!" His arms still held the pillow in place.

"The beard," she said. "F.X., where's the beard? Okay, that's enough. You can let go now."

"What?"

"I said, you can let go now."

"The beard's over there . . ."

"Let go," she demanded. Then, as he whispered something in her ear, she said again—without much conviction this time, though—"You can let go now."

His hands still about her waist, he worked loose the pillow and tossed it to the ground.

With the pillow cushioning her head she lay on the damp earth, worried that one of the children might wander outside and see them, that Burma or Mr. Randy might come looking for her. But she didn't stop him when he unbuttoned her jacket and pulled down the ridiculous pants. As he mounted her his breath stirred the down on her cheeks, which were gaudy pink with helpless love.

"Donna Lee, Donna Lee . . ." he said while the image of that black child taunting her was swallowed up in merciful darkness.

CHAPTER

Thirty-four

Mr. Pickens got up off the love seat, where he was eating a can of warmed-up chop suey, and went to the bathroom to inspect the progress of his black eye. It wasn't Emmet who had given him the shiner—it looked much darker now, he observed, peering at himself in the medicine-cabinet mirror— but Miss Mina. She had come running out of the house to break up the fight, and hit him in the eye with a SqeeGee mop. She made Emmet and him set up the manger exactly as it had been before. Then, without giving Mr. Pickens a chance to explain that he was only there for a little gas, she threw them both off her property.

"You done ruined my life," Emmet had said as he siphoned gas from his car into the yellow Chevette's tank. Standing on the highway, Emmet seemed small and helpless, and his nose was bleeding. Mr. Pickens suffered a pang of fatherly concern and tried to wipe the blood away with his handkerchief.

"Ain't it enough you ruined me and Burma?" Emmet said,

grabbing the handkerchief and throwing it into the weed-choked ditch. "Now you got to ruin my Christmas Eve too."

Mr. Pickens tried to explain that he had only gone to Miss Mina's for gas and that he had no idea Emmet would be there, but Emmet wouldn't listen. He said he had endured enough to last him a lifetime, and furthermore he didn't want any of Mr. Pickens's filthy money. (Mr. Pickens had offered him five dollars for the gas.) All he wanted was to get clear of Bobby (Carl, Mr. Pickens corrected), Carl, whatever his blasted name was. So Emmet Orney got in his car and gunned it north to Vicksburg. He vowed he'd never set foot in Louisiana again as long as he lived.

Mr. Pickens went back to his supper in the living room. The fight had left him thoughtful, reflective. It was the first real fight he had ever been in—one, that is, where he had actually returned a few punches himself. Looking at his swollen, bruised knuckles, he confirmed his initial surprise that it hurt more to hit than to be hit. Somehow this didn't seem right. Another thing that troubled him was Emmet's behavior after the fight. The more he mulled it over, the stranger it seemed that Emmet had offered to give him gas. If he was really that angry, why hadn't he left Mr. Pickens stranded on the highway? Could it be that Emmet felt a little guilty about Burma? Maybe that was the reason Emmet couldn't get it through his thick head that Mr. Pickens didn't love her. Maybe all along Emmet *wanted* Mr. Pickens to love her, so he, Emmet, could be free. But how could Mr. Pickens love someone like that? She was fine as a friend. In fact, he used to like her a lot until everything was ruined by his moronic striptease at Josie Wayne. After that it was impossible to think of her as just a friend; but neither could he imagine her as a lover—unless, of course, he was drunk. Only then did her looks not seem so important.

Oh, Lord, would he ever understand anything about love? Maybe if he became an alcoholic, then everything would be solved.

Ever since returning from Miss Mina's, Mr. Pickens was nagged by a feeling that he had forgotten to do something. He put down his fork, which was laden with beansprouts. That's right, he was supposed to kill himself. But for some reason he didn't feel like doing it anymore. He had gone through enough excitement for one evening.

He sighed and picked up his fork.

He put the fork down again.

The watch.

His appetite vanished. It was one thing to give a perfect stranger a $489.43 watch when you thought you weren't going to be around to pay the monthly installments on it. However, now that he planned to go on living . . . What if he told the jewelers he had lost the watch? He'd still have to pay for it— even if it was stolen. He had no theft insurance, nothing to cover things being lost, either. Then should he go back to the Sugar Shack? But the ice-cream girl would surely put up a big fuss. And who could blame her? It was undoubtedly the best Christmas present anyone had ever given her. And she seemed tough. What if she called the sheriff's office and made up some story about him trying to entice her with the watch, seduce her? She was underage too, maybe only thirteen, twelve. He couldn't bear the thought of getting involved with the police again, trying to explain something that looked so fishy. How was it that a man who had never broken the law, who believed in the law with his whole heart, was always on the verge of being arrested? And how could this same man, who really appreciated good looks in a woman, spend so much time wondering about an overweight thirty-seven-year-old who didn't know the first thing about makeup? Mr. Pickens sank down onto the love seat and buried his face in a needlepoint cushion.

"Hey, son, wake up."

Mr. Pickens raised his head from the cushion and saw F.X. standing in the front hall. He was stepping out of the red pants of his Santa suit.

"Sleeping on Christmas Eve," F.X. chided and, beaming good-naturedly, aimed Santa's belly, the pillow, right at his brother. It hit Mr. Pickens on his left arm, which was numb and just beginning to prickle awake; he had slept on it.

"I wasn't sleeping," Mr. Pickens said, rubbing a red zigzag pattern that his cheek had picked up from the cushion.

"What happened to your eye?" F.X. asked as he disappeared into the bedroom down the hall.

"Nothing, I just . . . "

F.X. came out a few moments later, dressed in jeans, boots, and a new cowboy shirt. "How do you like it?" He held out his arms so the shirt could be admired. Then, seeing the chop suey, he said, "What's this muck doing here?"

"It's my supper."

"Dump it, son. We're going over to the Keelys'. There's plenty of food there."

"What?"

"Josie Wayne's poisoned. Donna Lee didn't want us staying out there any longer, so she herded us all over to her parents'. They got a big place, you know. This fat dude Mr. Randy's there, Moab, Burma, and there's all these little kids you can play with. Come on."

Burma—there she was again, disturbing the little peace he had found by relinquishing the watch. Mr. Pickens folded his arms across his chest. "You can't go there, F.X."

"To the Keelys'? Why not? She asked me herself just a

minute ago, Mrs. Keely did. Shit, you should've seen her, poor lady. Trying so hard to smile and be nice. A real tight-ass, but hell, she'll make it, I guess."

"If you had any sense of decency—"

F.X. looked at Mr. Pickens's face, and suddenly his own face mirrored that anger, that doubt. "What? If I had any decency, I'd stay home? Is that it?"

"Yes, that's right."

The two brothers stood there a moment in the dim, cramped living room that was their home. Looking down at that damn plastic-covered love seat, Mr. Pickens felt that no one could ever understand his bitterness and defeat. But then, glancing over at his brother's face, he saw written there, in eyes black with pain, a story that was somehow like his own.

"F.X.," Mr. Pickens said after a long silence that nearly crushed them both, "I guess I'm ready now. Let's go."

As they were walking down the sidewalk that cut the front yard in half Mr. Pickens was suddenly overcome with doubt again. He stopped, gazing up at the stars. It hurt a lot to look at them, those shameless stars, but he couldn't help looking. Then he felt an arm around his shoulder—"Come on, son, they're waiting for us"—and with this yoke, which was easy, he was able to continue on his way.

For a complete list of books available from Penguin in the United States, write to Dept. DG, Penguin Books, 299 Murray Hill Parkway, East Rutherford, New Jersey 07073.

For a complete list of books available from Penguin in Canada, write to Penguin Books Canada Limited, 2801 John Street, Markham, Ontario L3R 1B4.